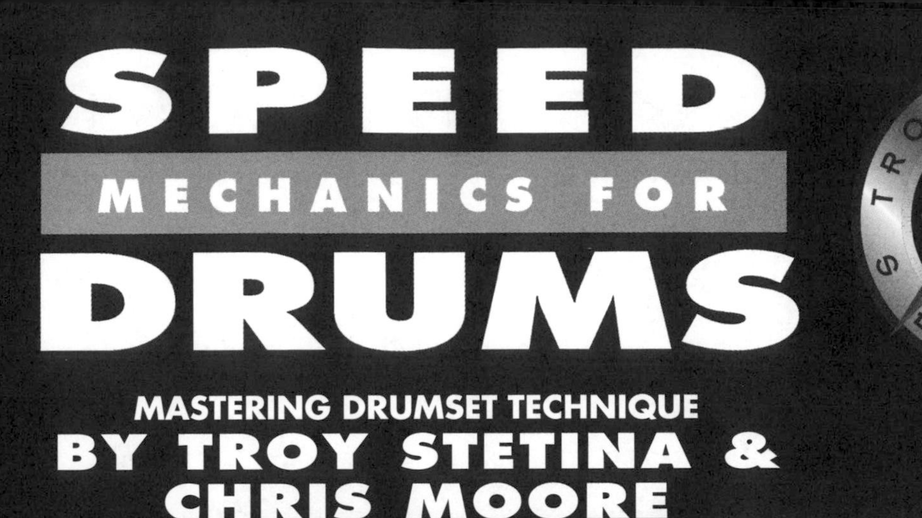

MASTERING DRUMSET TECHNIQUE

BY TROY STETINA & CHRIS MOORE

Guitars and Bass Played by Troy Stetina
Recorded by Troy Stetina
Mixed by Bob Daspit

To access video visit:
www.halleonard.com/mylibrary
Enter Code
4305-3854-9676-7072

ISBN 978-1-4950-0403-2

7777 W. BLUEMOUND RD. P.O. BOX 13819 MILWAUKEE, WI 53213

In Australia Contact:
Hal Leonard Australia Pty. Ltd.
4 Lentara Court
Cheltenham, Victoria, 3192 Australia
Email: ausadmin@halleonard.com.au

www.stetina.com

Visit Hal Leonard Online at
www.halleonard.com

CONTENTS

ABOUT THE AUTHORS

CHRIS MOORE is a professional studio drummer who has performed on many CDs, singles, commercials, and soundtracks for artists, bands, and producers all around the world. He is also a member of the band Endangered Species, and regularly performs with Damage and other independent artists. In October 2014, Chris wrote and released a single with Angelo Moore of Fishbone called "Curse of 1000 Mommies." He is known for his ability to combine speed, power, and groove on the drums. Chris endorses ddrum, Ahead drumsticks, Aquarian drumheads, Axis bass drum pedals, and TRX cymbals. Check out his website **www.ChrisMooreDrums.com** for live performance schedules and samples of his work.

TROY STETINA is an internationally recognized guitarist and music educator, and author of *Speed Mechanics for Lead Guitar*—the first method to look deeply into the principles of lead guitar technique, to break it down into its component skills, perfect those skills, and reassemble them to attain a level of mastery. He has written more than forty methods for Hal Leonard Corporation, and has released CDs as a solo artist and with his former band Second Soul. Troy endorses Dimis guitars, PRS guitars, Engl amps, and Dunlop strings and picks. He also co-owns sheet music retailer Music44.com, as well as online retailers Chai-Direct.com, Single-Serve-Direct.com, and Lampifier Microphones, where he manages artist relations. Visit him online at **www.TroyStetina.com** for lessons, music, and events.

PREFACE

This book is written for anyone who wants to improve their drumming—most commonly intermediate to advanced players who want to brush up on their skills and take them up a notch. Those who have played for some time but perhaps have not taken it as seriously as they would have liked will find this method to be of immense benefit, as it will direct them to exactly what and how to practice to reap solid rewards. Specific knowledge, such as reading drum notation, while helpful, is not necessary.

If you are a beginner, you also need to learn this material, but a word of caution: This is not a beginner method, and many techniques here can take years to master. Take a long term view, therefore, and expect to progress slowly, perhaps using this book to supplement a more gradual, standard method. This method is for those who want to break barriers and push into new territory. It is a method for drummers who want to be challenged; who want to be the best they can be.

Regardless of your level, however, if you are willing to work hard and embrace the concepts presented here, this book will undoubtedly help you accomplish both your drumming goals and your musical goals. These pages are a guide to playing the drumset faster, stronger, smoother, and cleaner. And as you improve your speed and skills, you will be removing any barriers that may stand between you and the perfection of your music.

Drumming involves a complex set of skills. By breaking them down into their components and developing each skill individually in a highly efficient manner, then reassembling them, you will find that you gain not only speed, but also accuracy, strength, stamina, control, fluency of execution, and even greater creativity! There is no limit to what you can do with the right approaches.

This is also a book you can continue to use for years, because as good as you get, you can always hone your skills further and evolve new musical applications. You can refer back to this book whenever you want to refresh your skills, or if you're feeling stuck. At certain times, most everyone experiences plateaus. Whenever that happens, you can be sure that the trouble lies in one or more fundamental skills that are not yet fully mastered. Use what you learn here to drill deeper into those basics and identify your problem areas so you can blast through whatever limitations you may be facing.

With a title like *Speed Mechanics for Drums*, it may appear that this book is all about double bass (given the fact that "speed styles" of drumming tend to utilize a lot of double bass), but this book lays out a holistic approach to drumming. Here you will be developing both hand speed and control as well as foot speed and control, and integrating them together. Equal focus on the hands will take your playing to even more exciting levels, and we will explore how to use your newfound speed skills to create highlight moments in songs and fills that "jump out" in the mix. We will also explore the importance of keeping a cooperative mindset—really listening to and playing *with* the musicians in your band or project.

Years ago, I played in a thrash metal band with a famous singer who was creating songs that required double bass at 170 bpm–200 bpm for four minutes at a time, usually with little or no rest. I had to step up or lose the gig, so I made it my goal to play 200 bpm for four minutes straight without fading. In achieving that goal, however, my hand skills suffered. Then just at that moment, I was referred to a much bigger band for a position as their touring drummer. I lost out on that opportunity because they had a grooving rock vibe and my double bass focus did not fit their sound. Placing all my focus on my foot skills cost me the gig!

Being a well-rounded drummer is vitally important. As a studio musician, in fact, I've never been hired for a recording session in which I was asked to play fast double bass, although I have been told many times specifically *not to*! In the recording world, the hands are just as important, if not more important, than the feet. It's about groove and feel, and that involves both hands and feet, integrated. Groove and feel can never be sacrificed. And yet, speed matters too, because when it's called for, you want to execute it reliably and flawlessly within the context of that groove.

It's also worth noting that I'm a hard hitter who plays the drums with a lot of passion and movement. And my teaching approach is based on the way I play. But this is not the *only* way to play. If you have a different feel of playing and prefer to simply adapt some of the ideas presented here into your own style, I would encourage you to do just that—apply what feels right for you.

The real goal here is to take what you learn from this book to become the drummer *you* dream of being. So of course you have the final say in adapting these principles, whether that means transforming yourself into a double bass ninja, or a fast, clean, all-around drumset artist, I wish you success on that path. The purpose here is to give you the tools to master whatever skill set you need to create your own unique artistic vision.

—Chris Moore

INTRODUCTION

 INTRODUCTION VIDEO

IT'S ALL ABOUT PRACTICE

The drumming concepts and exercises in these pages will undoubtedly place you on the path to faster and cleaner playing—but it's all up to you to put in the time and effort to make it happen. What is the secret to playing fast and playing well? It is simple: *Practice*. There is no magic you can apply or shortcut you can take; you just have to put the time into your craft. The best you can hope for is to apply yourself effectively and efficiently, and get the most out of your practice time. I will give you clear guidance on how to do that. But it's up to you to actually put in the required time and *do it*.

It can be tempting at times to jump ahead and play faster than you are capable, but you need to do the work first or your technique will be inconsistent. The good news is, the more you practice these techniques and mechanics, the quicker you'll reach your drumming goals. Think of it like driving to a destination: the only way to get there is to actually drive the car. You have to be actively involved in the process; don't wait for the car to drive itself or you'll never get there. It's the same thing here. The more actively involved you get in developing your skills, the closer you'll be to rippin' that double bass run you never thought you could play, or flying around the toms, your hands nothing but a blur!

Question: How much, exactly, should you practice? Consider the adage: "good" practices until you get it right; "great" practices until you can't get it wrong! I'm going to encourage you to seek the latter.

LEARN TO RELAX

Another "secret" is this: The more relaxed you are, the faster you can play. It's a natural response to try to control our bodies by *forcing* ourselves to play faster. When that happens, we tighten up and this actually introduces a barrier, or speed limit. It also inhibits the flow and evenness of execution that is so important, and we risk injuring ourselves when our muscles are tight and not fluid. So relax! Take a moment to breathe and allow your body to move rather than forcing it.

If you're pushing yourself too hard by forcing, you will find yourself playing choppy. How tight is your back? How tense are your arms? Back off your metronome bpm (beats per minute) just a little. As you slow it down, become aware of how your body *feels* as you play these exercises. Pay more attention to the internal feel and less to the external measurement of speed. Get your flow going right, in a more relaxed space, and you will find yourself able to increase the tempo almost effortlessly. It is this sensation you want to maintain as you work up to your speed goals.

THE IMPORTANCE OF WARMING UP

The drumset is a physically demanding instrument and your body is always changing and adapting to it. Some days you may require very little warm-up to reach your target speed. Other days it may take an hour or more. It differs based on several factors, including how fatigued your muscles are, how much you've eaten, what you've eaten, how much sleep you got, the temperature in the room, how stressed you are, etc. Take your time in warming up and always relax into your drumming. Accept where you are at any given moment and *work with your body*, rather than trying to force it.

In preparing to write and record the challenge-song "Kaleidoscope," which appears at the end of this book, I spent between one to two hours warming up each day. The process of writing and recording the song took about two weeks. Certainly, coming up with the various drum parts and a song structure that applied everything in this book was a complex task. Yet, the *real work* came when I actually recorded it. Every time I wanted to work on this song, I had to commit to the process of warming up and getting into "that place" before I could really get productive. When I tried to hurry through my warm-up, my playing became more inconsistent—relatively sloppy and just not at the level needed for such a high-level drum-challenge piece. This led to a great deal of frustration and even some soul searching. After all, I really wanted to create a personal best here. Getting honest with myself, I had to recognize at those times that I just hadn't put in the required time and I was trying to rush the process to "get it done." But staying focused on the quality of the end result was the big motivator, and I couldn't shortcut it. The recording told the truth. In fact, there were a few times when I just had to stop recording altogether and go back to warming up all over again, to pull it off the way I *knew* I could. *Then* everything flowed. And there were also times when life interrupted—I had to finish recording a track for another artist, get something to eat, pick up my son from school, etc.—and when I got back into the studio, you guessed it... I had to start the whole warm-up process over. You simply cannot play your best without an adequate warm-up.

This is just as true for a live show as it is in the studio. It is always vital that you take some time alone to center yourself and get your muscles ready for what is to come. Several years ago, I was playing with a high-energy band that went onstage in full blast mode. At that point, I hadn't yet discovered the value of warming up before going onstage. Because I was walking out there physically and mentally unprepared, I found myself playing catch-up throughout the entire set! It would have been so much better to be in control and "in the moment" rather than reacting to what was happening. It requires commitment and patience, but to produce your best, it is essential.

ENJOY THE JOURNEY!

When you're working toward something specific, your focus may shift to become primarily on the end result. Then it is a short step to becoming very dissatisfied that you are not at your goal *right now*. Our society is very results-driven, very outcome-oriented. If you are of the mindset that you will be happy only when you achieve this or have that, you are really setting yourself up for misery, and you will burn out. Trust me, I've done it. Slow down and enjoy the ride!

Know that every step of your journey is taking you in the direction of your goal, though it may not seem like it sometimes. In retrospect, however, this can always be seen to have been true. So relish the good times *and* the difficult times. Enjoy your path to success. Enjoy your practice time. Enjoy where you are right now, and stay present within *this* step. Ironically, this makes you better, because as you enjoy it, this quality will tend to come through in everything you do, including (especially) your drumming. I'm not saying you shouldn't be ambitious. I'm suggesting that you apply your ambition toward choosing to practice regularly, choosing to focus on the right things as you practice, being consistent, and continuing to grow as a musician day by day and enjoying the process!

ARTISTRY IN DRUMMING

I don't claim to be the fastest drummer out there, nor do I strive for that. Rather, I use speed as a tool to create exciting moments in songs. That's where I've found it to be most effective. What has gotten me hired for recording gigs and live shows is the ability to groove, to lock in with a band, and to be a team player. Of course, there are moments to jump out and shine; the key, in my opinion, is to choose those moments wisely, and make your mark in a way that also serves the song.

I once took a drum lesson from Bernie Dresel. Bernie played with The Brian Setzer Orchestra and is one of my favorite drummers of all time. He has amazing swing in his playing, and can also play a funk groove like you wouldn't believe. He even grooves while he plays fast. Bernie plays ahead of himself, but is always very much in the moment. In other words, he prepares himself for what's coming up in the song so he can flawlessly execute his chops.

During our lesson, I brought up the subject of playing fast. Bernie told me about a drummer he had recently seen on TV. That drummer played something really fast and Bernie said, "Wow! Look at that!" The drummer did it again and Bernie thought, "Pretty cool." The drummer did it a third time and Bernie changed the channel. His point was that, even though he's a drummer, he's also a listener just like everybody else. Too much of a good thing can get tiresome, and the drummer he was watching could have made a much bigger impact by doing his fast drum trick once, then moving on and allowing the audience to still be saying, "Wow! Did you see that?"

As an artist, I feel there is a time and place to play fast, and I apply it as it feels right and in balance, listening to the needs of the song (and style) and the other players. Often you can gauge your playing by how the other musicians react to what you're doing. They may give you (or each other) a look, which lets you know if you're on the right track. They may comment on your playing after the song ends. Take those cues and adjust accordingly. I've experienced both sides: where the musical director or other musicians have told me to hold back just a bit, and where they have encouraged me to give it "more of that"—which is, of course, more fun! The important thing here is to use your instinct and work with the band, for the sake of the song. You are, after all, a member of a team of musicians here working together. So be a part of that team, and listen and be responsive.

If you're looking to make a living as a studio musician or live performer on tour, it is important to realize that fast won't be the primary skill for which most artists and producers are looking. A great example is Tony Royster, Jr., who is another favorite drummer of mine, and a huge influence. Tony is incredibly fast with hands *and* feet, but when he got the gig with Jay Z, it was because of his amazing groove. Sure, he can bring the chops when needed, but he's primarily there to hold down the big beat. *The ideal is to be able to play any speed you want, cleanly and with a rock solid groove.* And that is what this method will help you achieve.

DRUM NOTATION

The drum notation staff shows which drums and cymbals are to be hit, and when. If you are not already familiar with the drum staff, take a moment now and look it over. It is pretty straightforward. The different "note" positions on the staff vertically correspond to the different drums and cymbals.

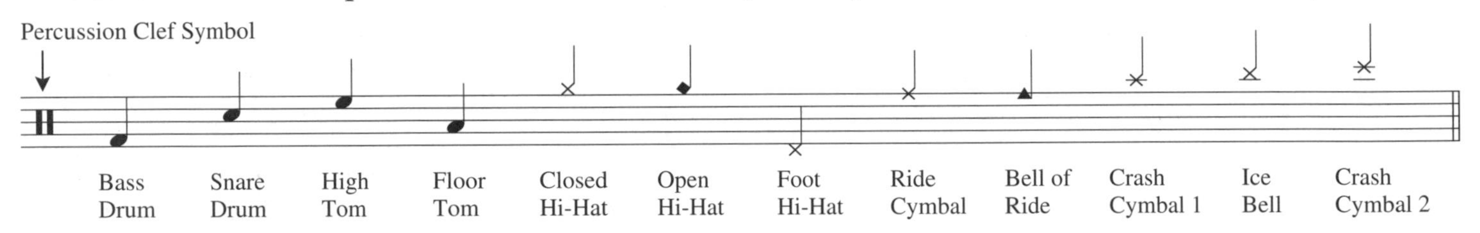

Next, there is the timing aspect to consider. 4/4 ("four-four") time is the most common time signature. This means that the music is separated into short segments called *measures* with four beats in each measure. So a quarter of a measure, or *quarter note*, gets one beat. Hits that occur at double the speed of the pulse (or beat, or click) are *eighth notes*, which are joined by a beam. Sixteenth notes are twice as fast as eighths, which means they are four notes per beat. These are indicated with a double beam.

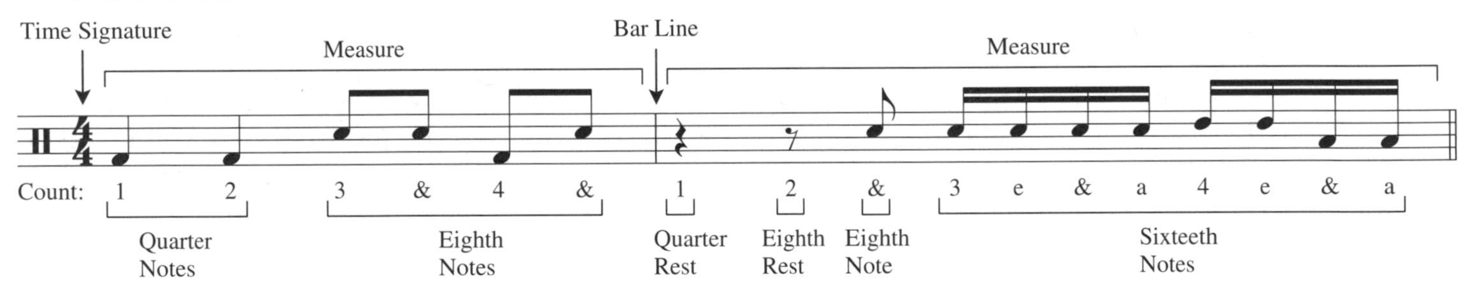

The rhythm "pyramids" below give a sense of the relationship between different note durations. Notes (hits) are on the left. Rests (spaces of silence) are on the right.

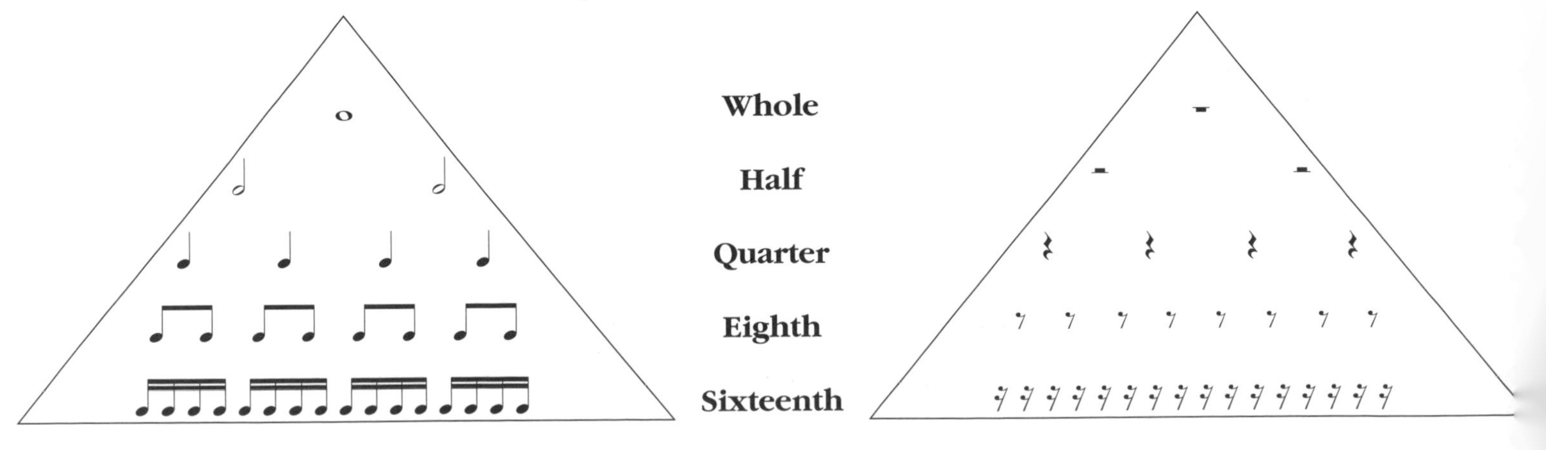

If you are unfamiliar with the notation of rhythm, that's okay. As you progress through the video and listen to the examples, follow along with the notation and it will all start to fall into place.

DRUMKIT SETUP

Principles for Arranging Your Kit

There are many ways to arrange a set of drums. What's most important is that you set up your kit for your own comfort. You should be able to reach every piece without straining or stretching. Imagine the countless hours of practice, playing, recording, and the repetitive motion involved in drumming on a regular basis. I've heard stories of drummers being sidelined during tours by playing injury. My guess is that in most cases, their drums were not set up properly. The repetitive motion of playing hard night after night can wreak havoc on muscles, joints, and tendons. So we need to make sure our drums are set up in such a way that we can spend hours at a time playing without worrying about causing extra fatigue and/or strain injuries.

Sit down at your drumset and close your eyes. Visualize where you want each drum and cymbal to be, then arrange your kit based on that, keeping these three principles in mind:

- You should be able to reach every drum and cymbal comfortably.
- You should be able to close your eyes and know where everything is on your kit.
- You should be able to play for hours at a time without strain on your joints or tendons.

A lot of drummers ask about distances between drums, cymbal height, and drum stool height. If your drums or cymbals are set too close to you, they can get in the way and cause bruises and cuts on your hands. Too far away, and you risk injury to your muscles, joints, and tendons. Again, the most important thing here is comfort.

Viewed from the Front

Viewed from the Drummer's Left

Viewed from the Drummer's Right

Viewed from Above

Distance Between Drums

The distance between your drums is really a matter of preference. In terms of speed mechanics, you should be able to get from one tom to the next without the distance interrupting your flow. It should also be noted that the height and angle of each drum is based upon comfort and ease of play. I've seen drummers place a single rack tom high and flat in front of them so they have to reach upward in order to play it. Any hits on a tom in that position would either have to be rimshots or they'd be very soft in comparison to the rest of the kit. In contrast, some drummers place their drums at sharp angles so their sticks glance off the drumheads. This setup might look cool, but it's not functional and probably doesn't sound very good, since the power of each drum stroke is compromised by not directing the force of the stroke directly into the drumhead.

Cymbal Height

Cymbal height can be a little more complex than you might think. First and foremost, comfort is the key. You should also consider the overall sound quality of your drumset, in terms of microphone placement for recording and live performances. If the cymbals are too low, their sound may bleed into your tom mics. If they're too high, your overhead mics may be placed too high and not capture the rest of the kit as intended. The other consideration with high cymbal placement as it relates to speed mechanics, is that the distance between cymbals and drums is greater and can slow down your playing as you attempt to get around the kit. As always, comfort should win out on this one. Years ago, I placed my cymbals high, but lowered them for the reasons just listed. One of my drum heroes developed a shoulder injury as a result of reaching up for his cymbals and it made me reconsider the importance of cymbal placement.

Drum Stool Height

Above all, the most important thing here is, you guessed it… comfort! I've played with my drum stool high, low, and everywhere in between. There are many different theories on this subject, but the most popular position appears to be when your thighs are parallel with the floor. Posture is very important in drumming, so you want to sit up with your back straight and the drum stool supporting your upper body. Place your stool so you are close enough to the kit and you don't have to bend over to reach your rack tom(s). Your pedals should be set so your lower leg is just about perpendicular to the floor. You want to be close enough that you can apply downward pressure that originates in your hips, and not so far out that the pressure has to come from your knees. This will give your kick more power and will help prevent injuries to your knees.

PART ONE

BUILDING SPEED AND CONTROL

In this section, we will increase hand speed, consistency, and control first on single drum exercises, then we will move it around the kit. After that, we will examine the mechanics of your foot work. Success always traces back to mastery of the fundamentals, so that is where we begin…

HANDS

PREPARATION VIDEO A

Use Heavy Drumsticks to Build Strength

Using a pair of heavy drumsticks during practice will help you build muscle strength faster in these initial exercises. Similar to the idea of lifting weights when in training to swing a baseball bat or golf club better, heavy practice sticks will help increase your strength and stamina for drumming. The stronger you are, the more you can relax as you play, and therefore, the faster you will be able to play. For building hand speed and control, we will do exercises 1-5 on a practice pad with heavy drumsticks.

I use Ahead Drumsticks exclusively. When on the practice pad, I use their Work Out sticks; while on the drumset, I use their Tommy Lee Studio sticks. Ahead Drumsticks are more durable than most sticks because they're made of an alloy core on the inside, covered by a polyurethane sleeve on the outside. Since I'm a hard hitter, I broke a lot of wood sticks before I discovered Ahead Drumsticks. I also like to wrap the handles of my sticks with white athletic tape, which keeps them from slipping, and provides a nice cushion from the vibration of playing hard.

As for the practice pad itself, I like the Aquarian Super Pad. It fits on the snare drum nicely and provides an honest feel when you play it. Many practice pads are made of rubber and don't give a drum-like feel when you play on them. But the Aquarian Super Pad actually feels like you're playing the real drum, and you can even hear the snare drum as you're playing, since it is constructed to allow muted drum tones to flow through.

PREPARATION VIDEO B

Match Grip

As far as grip and technique, I prefer match grip using the Moeller method, also known as the Moeller technique. If you want to look into it further, there are plenty of interpretations of the Moeller method online.

Here is a brief description of how I use it.

- Keep your elbows in, close to your sides.
- Grip the bottom end of the stick with your pinky finger and ring finger, which will be the primary drivers of your drum stroke.
- Your middle finger, index finger, and thumb are there to guide the stick and add control to your drum strokes.
- Hold your pinky and ring finger around the stick, then turn your hand in so your thumb is on the side, facing inward toward your other hand.
- The sensation you're going for is a "whipping motion" that allows gravity to do most of the work.
- Relax your muscles and allow the drum stroke to start at the bottom of the stick where your pinky finger and ring finger are delivering the power. Feel that whipping motion as you contract those fingers on the down stroke. Your muscles must be relaxed to allow this motion to be fluid.

You can watch me demonstrate this motion on the accompanying video. Where you'll really start to feel it during practice is in your forearms, because those are the muscles that originate the drum stroke.

If you choose to study this method in detail, there are entire books on the subject. The truth is, I believe that if a given technique works for you, you'll perfect it in the doing of it, making the necessary adjustments in order that your technique will adapt and fit into your playing style. So feel free to adapt this method as it feels right for you. As long as you are relaxed and not feeling pain anywhere, you are on the right track.

PREPARATION VIDEO C

The Metronome

The use of a metronome is vital to your progress as a drummer. Most professional drummers use a metronome (or "click") for practice, rehearsal, recording, and live shows. A metronome will help you deliver a solid tempo in any situation you encounter, and this is critical. So it is vitally important that you become accustomed to and comfortable with playing to the metronome. We measure the speed of the metronome in bpm or "beats per minute," so 60 bpm means 60 beats per minute (or one beat per second). In this case, we say that the *tempo* of the clock is 60 bpm.

The metronome is also a great tool for setting practice goals, working toward those goals, and measuring your progress along the way. Let's suppose you have a song that is at 170 bpm and you want to do a fill in sixteenth-note triplets. That is very fast, and you'll probably need to work up to that kind of hand speed a little at a time with the help of a metronome. In fact, to hit such a speed reliably and without excess tension within a song, you will probably find that you will need to be able to hit even *higher* tempos with the metronome in your practice sessions.

There are several metronome apps for smartphones that you can download for little or no cost. If you don't have a smartphone, buy a metronome online or at your local music store.

Hand Mechanics on a Single Drum

Our first mechanic will be the one I use at the beginning of my warm-up. It is played all on the snare. Always use a metronome. On the video I demonstrate each example at four speeds to give you an idea of how this looks and sounds at varying tempos. You should always begin slowly, at a manageable tempo, and then increase by 10–20 bpm at a time, once you are feeling comfortable and proficient at each tempo. Feel the muscles working in your forearms and remember to relax, especially at higher speeds where tension has a way of unconsciously creeping in.

When you reach a tempo at which you feel you must force it, back off a few bpm until you can regain that relaxed feeling. Then increase the tempo, maintaining that feel.

EXAMPLE VIDEO 1

Hand Exercise 1: Alternating Hands Every Four Strokes

The next exercise stretches out the number of drum strokes for each hand before alternating, which works the muscles and builds strength. This is where using heavier sticks for practice begins to pay off. Again, always use the metronome.

EXAMPLE VIDEO 2

Hand Exercise 2: Alternating Hands Every Eight Strokes

R R R R R R R R L L L L L L L L

Once you've mastered Exercises 1 and 2, it's time to put your muscles to the test for Exercises 3 and 4. See how many bars you can play with each hand at a moderate tempo. I've spent countless hours doing these single-hand mechanics. There have actually been days where I did nothing but play these on a practice pad; no alternating, no drumset, no fun! But I did get much stronger and played far better and with greater control afterward. Make no mistake, these exercises will pay big dividends toward your technique and control.

Hand Exercise 3a: Single Hand, Right

Hand Exercise 3b: Single Hand, Left

Now, as you're building strength in each hand with the above exercises, let's also focus on dexterity and control. Keep your drum strokes even, both in terms of spacing in time and in volume (velocity) of each hit. Make each hit sound the same, as though you're doing it all with one hand. Don't worry about sounding too much like a drum machine. At this point we are using this mechanic to build strength, control, and speed. Start at a manageable tempo and gradually increase your bpm. Remember to avoid holding excess tension. The more you relax, the faster you can play!

If your drum strokes become uneven, it most likely means that you're tightening up and trying to play too fast, too soon. Slow down, back off your bpm just a bit, relax, and go at it again.

Hand Exercise 4: Alternating Hands Every Stroke

Moving Around the Kit

Ready to move around the kit? The mechanics that follow build on what you've just worked on with single strokes by taking it between the snare drum, rack tom, and floor tom. But first, let's cover a few important concepts. When moving around the drumset, always remember this: *Make sure your hands get there first.*

What I mean is, get your hands in position before you execute your drum strokes. This will improve your accuracy and allow you to play cleaner and with more consistency. Seems logical, but it's easier said than done. Most drummers begin their drum strokes while their hands are traveling between the drums. This leads to sloppy drumming and inconsistent hits. It's just like taking a shot in basketball; your accuracy will be much better when you're in a set position than when you're moving. Terry Bozzio is probably the best drummer I've seen utilize this concept. If you watch him play, you will see that his hands are always in place over the drums as he begins his drum strokes. He plays a massive kit and is incredibly clean in his playing.

"Hands get there first..."

Why is accuracy and consistency so important? Creating a professional sound on the drums involves knowing how and where to hit each drum. Striking the drums and cymbals in the "sweet spot" takes focus and lots of practice. As you develop this skill, it becomes second nature and allows you to *pull* your chosen sound out of the drumset. You may have heard the expression, "It's in the hands." This means that the tone doesn't just come from the instrument itself, it comes from the musician playing it.

I once sat next to Eddie Van Halen in the dressing room while he warmed up for a concert. Looking at his famous red, white, and black striped "Frankenstein" guitar, you'd never think it would sound good. It was thrashed, with wires hanging out and rust covering some of the metal parts. He plugged it straight into a Fender Champ amplifier and BOOM...there was that unmistakable sound. If someone else played his guitar, there's no way it would sound the same. Eddie's tone is in his hands. And it's the same with drumming. I remember playing a show in which the drummers of all the bands on the bill shared the same kit. Vinnie Appice was one of those playing that night. As soon as he sat down, I recognized his sound. It was the *same drumset*, using the *same tuning* as everyone else, but a different tone came through because of the musician that he is, exactly how and where he hits. *Tone really is in the technique.*

As you progress through the exercises in this book, think about developing your own sound, your own tone. Focus on getting your hands where they need to be before you begin your drum strokes. Watch how my hands move around the kit in the videos and you'll see that a big part of my sound is getting my hands into position before I actually hit each drum. This preparation allows for solid, accurate hits that really count. And that translates into the overall tone I pull from the drumset. It's the difference between merely hitting the drums and actually playing music.

"Tone is in the technique..."

In the next exercise, use alternating drum strokes starting on the snare drum, then move up to the rack tom, down to the floor tom, and back to the snare. Throughout this exercise, make your mantra *hands get there first*. Remind yourself of this simple phrase often, especially if you notice your playing is getting sloppy or you find yourself missing the sweet spot on each drum as you play.

Hand Exercise 5: Alternating Strokes, Variation 1

Now we will use the same format, but let's switch up the order of the drums you're hitting. In this exercise, you'll start on the snare, then go up to the rack tom, back to the snare, and then down to the floor tom. You will notice that changing the order of the drums provides a completely different experience in terms of sound and feel. Don't worry about using accents at this point, just work on getting your hands around the kit and making clean, solid hits on the drums. And of course, *hands get there first*.

EXAMPLE VIDEO 6

Hand Exercise 6: Alternating Strokes, Variation 2

Doubling Up

Now we will continue with alternating hits, but this time with only two hits on the snare, rack tom, back to the snare, then down to the floor tom. As in Hand Exercises 5 and 6, remember that *hands get there first.* But now, obviously, we have to set it up for every two hits rather than every four, so this is a more advanced mechanic—you change to each new drum literally twice as much within the same amount of time. That means twice as much setup adjustment motions must be made within the same amount of time, as compared to the preceding mechanic.

Start off at a manageable bpm and gradually increase your speed by 10 bpm at a time. Be sure that you're not feeling any pain in your hands, wrists, arms, shoulders, or back. You may need to adjust the position of your snare, rack tom, and/or floor tom so that you feel comfortable moving quickly between the drums. The idea here is to build strength and speed, while maintaining a fluid motion from one drum to the other.

Hand Exercise 7: Alternating Strokes, Variation 3

A Word About Application and Muscle Memory

Each specific example I'm showing you here is presented as an "exercise," but keep in mind that it is really the underlying *mechanic*, or stroke pattern, that you are seeking to develop in each case. With slight alterations with regard to tempo and/or sequencing of the drums, each of these mechanics may be adapted into many different musical situations with ease.

The previous mechanic is one that I incorporated into my drum solo at 00:14 (see the "Chris Moore Drum Solo" video located in the Additional Material portion of the video). There I used a very simple pattern involving only the snare drum and floor tom. I also like to use this mechanic as an important drum fill in my playing generally, as I've found that moving between two drums that sound completely different like this can definitely make a drum fill stand out in the mix.

As you practice each of the exercises in this book, be aware that any of these may be used for fills and solo pieces, or they may sound interesting when played at different speeds. That's how this one wound up playing a significant role in my drum solo. I practiced it so much as an exercise that I was able to play it consistently well. One day I heard it recorded in a practice session and it caught my ear. Then, when I was looking for a few "attention-getting" moments to place at the beginning of my drum solo, I used this idea to build one of those phrases. As you play through your practice sessions, be aware that you can certainly use your exercises in your everyday drumming.

It's also important to realize that we are creating *muscle memory* through each exercise sequence. Muscle memory is really the name of the game here. This happens when you have done something so many times that you don't even have to think about it. You experience this every day doing common things like walking or driving a car, or maybe while playing video games or catching a ball. The conscious thinking aspect becomes less of a factor as instinct takes over, and you just naturally do what you're supposed to do. The same thing happens in drumming: The more you practice, the more these exercises (and their underlying mechanics) become second nature, and can be relied upon to be executed flawlessly, with no thought required. A drum fill comes up as you're playing along and your hands just fly as if on their own, and you realize that you just rolled through one of these mechanics effortlessly.

This is the point we want to reach, where your body knows how to do it without your mind having to *think* about it consciously. Here, instead of struggling with executing the drum part, you can do something much more useful—like putting your attention on the energy of the arrangement you are supporting! Now let's continue...

PREPARATION VIDEO E

Rimshot Accents

In Hand Exercise 8, focus on clean hits in the sweet spot on both drums. Use rimshots as you're performing this one. A rimshot happens when the middle of your drumstick hits the rim of the drum at the same time as the tip of your drumstick hits the center of the drumhead. The combination of these two hits at once creates a loud "pop!" and delivers that big rock snare drum sound that many of us seek. Think John Bonham. Rimshots add an important accenting dynamic into the playing of the drumset, and we will be using them in this method. As with any discipline, they simply require practice to get them sounding reliably the way you want.

For this exercise, I recommend you use rimshots on the snare if you're playing it slowly, and then move toward regular drum strokes as you increase your bmp. As always, relax and be sure your hands get there first!

EXAMPLE VIDEO 8

Hand Exercise 8: Alternating Strokes, Variation 4

Triplets Around the Kit

Triplets are three notes evenly spaced within a given time where normally two notes would appear. There are many ways to count triplets. You can count them as, "One-and-a, two-and-a, three-and-a, four-and-a" or you can count, "Trip-a-let, trip-a-let, trip-a-let, trip-a-let."

The mechanic in this exercise is another "drum chop" I use in my everyday playing. It helps to create an exciting moment that jumps out in the mix. Since it's in triplet form, it can go against the beat and become a very advanced drum fill. In the following example, we are hitting the snare drum on beats 1 and 3. As you build speed in this exercise, you'll find that it has a rhythmic feel all its own.

This exercise can build solid muscle memory, to the point where it becomes a "go to" drum fill in your playing. Stay loose and relaxed as you play this exercise. You will learn to trust that the hits naturally fall where they should through the physical movement of performing it. One thing I have to remember when I'm approaching this fill is to let go and just let it happen. If I try to control the hits, I usually miss. I have to just let my hands fly and allow muscle memory to take over. It takes a lot of practice to get to this point, but it's very much worth the effort.

Start off at a manageable bpm and increase your speed gradually. This is one of the most physically demanding exercises for your upper body, so approach it with care and make sure you're playing at a pace that feels comfortable for you.

EXAMPLE VIDEO 9

Hand Exercise 9: Triplets with Moving Voice, Snare on the Downbeat

And leading with the left:

And the "straight-ahead" variation, which is the same mechanic but presented in sixteenths.

And leading with the left hand:

Note: If you are right-handed, practice the right-hand versions first. (If you are a left, reverse this.) Then, after you have a handle on your preferred version, I encourage you also to try leading a bit with the other hand and see how that feels. It is good practice to shift out of your comfort zone and try things backwards once in a while, as that challenges your brain and body in a completely new way. Still, of course, you can always expect your dominant hand to lead with greater ease, and you will reach your highest speeds there.

To make it more advanced, we will now try placing the snare drum hits in places other than the downbeat of the triplet. Because the snare drum has a sound that stands out more than other drums, it has its own natural accent every time you hit it. This allows you to play the same basic idea but with the snare drum hits moved over, so to speak. You can mix it up any way you like to come up with a lot of interesting variations, but first try it in this format using triplets. Even though it is essentially the same motion, when it sits against the pulse differently, it feels very different.

Hand Exercise 10: Triplets with Snare on the Second Note

Hand Exercise 11: Triplets with Snare on the Third Note

PREPARATION VIDEO F

Double Strokes on a Single Drum

Double strokes are often overlooked by hard hitters because they don't pack the same punch as single strokes. However, they can be very well suited for fast stroke patterns at lower volume in intros and breakdowns. In fact, playing low-volume sixteenth-note single strokes at 100+ bpm can be a real challenge and can fatigue your muscles. In these situations it is much more efficient to play with double strokes. You can also use double strokes on the hi-hat during verses, or play double strokes on two different pieces of the drumkit.

Another interesting use for double strokes is to bring additional movement or texture to a song section or drum solo. Watch my drum solo video at 0:45–1:32 and you'll see I'm using double strokes in that section, but not as a breakdown; rather as an exposition of the central theme. This is an example of the use of double strokes executed with power.

In order to develop the strength to play them without sacrificing volume, I applied the Moeller method in terms of technique. It can be tempting to "cheat" when using double strokes by taking your pinky fingers and ring fingers off the sticks and letting your index fingers and thumbs do the work. However, this is where power, volume, and control are lost. Practice double strokes using the Moeller method to retain the power and volume needed both to control your double strokes and have them cut through the mix.

As with any drumming technique, the key to playing good double strokes is practice. Using heavy practice drumsticks, such as Ahead Drumsticks' "Work Out Sticks" will help you build strength and stamina. Start off on a practice pad at a manageable bpm tempo and increase gradually. Since this mechanic is based on strength and stamina, it is vital that you relax as you play it. Tightening up will only cause you to slow down and play choppy. Take the time to build your strength so you can relax and play with full control.

EXAMPLE VIDEO 12

Hand Exercise 12: Double Strokes on the Snare

Double Strokes Around the Kit

Moving around the drumset with double strokes takes lots of strength because you must retain the same power as you reach out further away from the snare drum. With your arms extended, it is much more difficult to play double strokes consistently, but it will come with practice.

For this next mechanic, work on maintaining your power while playing double strokes around the drumset. Relaxation is very important here. Pay attention to making your tone consistent. Listen to each hit and make it sound great!

Note: As you may have noticed in the previous triplet examples, the difference between leading with the right and leading with the left is that we are changing the repeating drum (high tom or floor tom) to avoid having to cross our arms awkwardly.

EXAMPLE VIDEO 13

Hand Exercise 13: Double Strokes Around the Kit, Variation 1

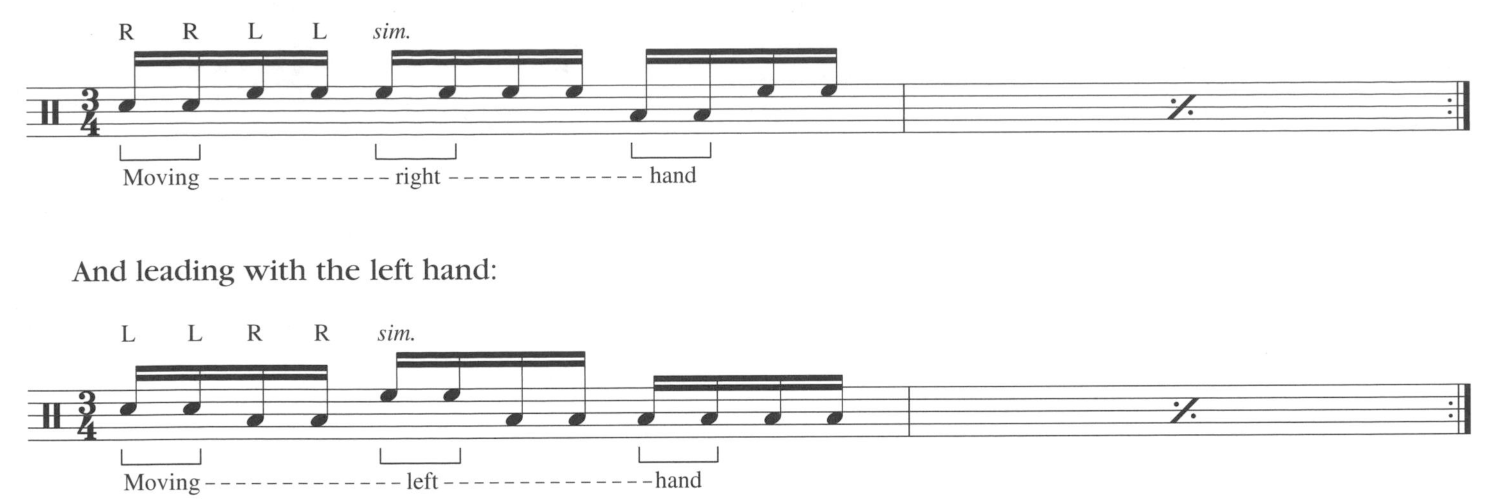

And leading with the left hand:

Now using the same approach, let's change the sequence of the drums we're hitting. Changing the order of the drums provides the listener with a different experience in terms of sound and feel. As with single strokes, work on getting your hands around the kit and making clean, solid hits on the drums. And just like with single strokes, *hands get there first*. The first part of Exercise 14 leads with the right hand, playing snare, rack tom, floor tom, then back to snare. Then try it leading with the left hand, which will be the weak hand for most of you. To accommodate left handed sticking without needing to cross your arms, notice that I have altered the pattern by reversing the last two drums. Feel free to experiment with other sequences as you move this idea around the kit.

EXAMPLE VIDEO 14

Hand Exercise 14: Double Strokes Around the Kit, Variation 2

The next mechanic is one of my favorite double-stroke fills to play on a drumset. We can use the same sticking pattern as we saw in Hand Exercise 8 but apply double strokes to it. As with Hand Exercise 8, we change drums every two hits rather than every four, so this is a more advanced mechanic. You must change to each new drum literally twice as often within the same amount of time—twice the setup adjustment, half as much time on each drum.

Start off at a manageable bpm and gradually increase your speed. Be sure that you don't feel any pain in your hands, wrists, arms, shoulders, or back. The idea here is to build strength and speed while maintaining a fluid motion from one drum to the other.

Hand Exercise 15: Double Strokes Around the Kit, Variation 3

And here is the same idea leading with the left hand. Again, although your non-dominant hand will probably never be as strong in the lead, there are often times when it can be beneficial to have the ability to reverse the sticking patterns.

The Six-Stroke Roll

The next mechanic incorporates the six-stroke roll, which I use in triplet form. Rolls have almost become a lost art in the world of rock and metal, because they are not as loud as single strokes and so have a tendency to "drop out" in a dense mix. But when used effectively, rolls can create unique moments within songs that work against the beat, build tension, and enhance transitions. Ian Paice used rolls in his work with Deep Purple and was one of the best-known drummers who applied this in a rock setting. John Bonham also had a vibe about his playing that gave a six-stroke roll feel to it, even when he was using single strokes. As you work through this mechanic, see if you can hear the influence of John Bonham or Ian Paice. And of course, *their* influence was the great Buddy Rich.

When I set out to learn the six-stroke roll, I was watching a video of John Bonham doing a drum solo that included some six-stroke roll work. I was fascinated and thought, "I don't think I could ever do that." But I learned that through practice, I surprised myself and eventually could play six-stroke rolls. In fact, it became one of my favorite disciplines in playing drums. I use the six-stroke roll in my drum solo video mentioned earlier, and am constantly looking for ways to incorporate it into new songs that I write and record.

The real key to playing rolls like this is *control*. You must control each individual hit. The drummer is responsible for every stroke within the roll. Some drummers just bounce the sticks off the drum in a kind of controlled chaos, guessing at which point to end the roll and hoping they come back in on the beat. This is not ideal. The proper way to play a roll is to know when each stroke is taking place, and *know that you know* you're coming back in on the beat. *Only when you have that confidence can you communicate that confidence, which is experienced by the listener as groove.*

Of course, the way to build such control is practice. You must practice this mechanic to the point where you can count along with it as easily as single strokes. Rolls require strength and power. Again, rather than *letting* the drumstick bounce off the drum, here you are actually *creating* the bounce for the drumstick.

The way you create the bounce for a six-stroke roll is through the use of accents. Your Moeller method is very important in creating the whipping motion for those accents. The sticking will be R-ll-rr-L-R, where the capitalized letters represent accents.

EXAMPLE VIDEO 16

Hand Exercise 16: Six-Stroke Roll

Begin slowly, and allow the sticks to bounce freely off the accents at first. Do these in short bursts, one round of R-ll-rr-L-R at a time. Pause after each one. As you speed up, gradually tighten your grip until you feel yourself controlling the bounce of the sticks. You can control how high each stick bounces so that you're "catching" the stick on the rebound upstroke from the accented downstroke and harnessing that energy for your next downstroke. Continue speeding up, and shorten your pauses until you are doing a continuous roll, like this:

EXAMPLE VIDEO 17

Hand Exercise 17: Continuous Six-Stroke Roll

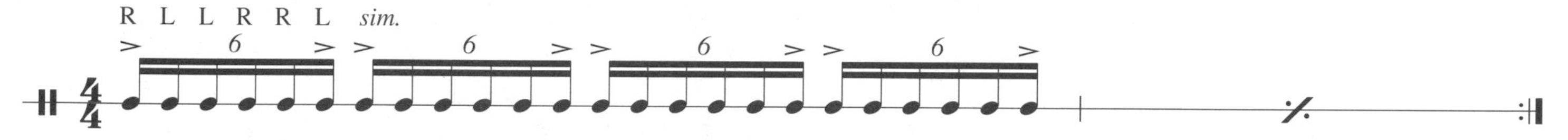

Next add hi-hat with the foot in eighth notes:

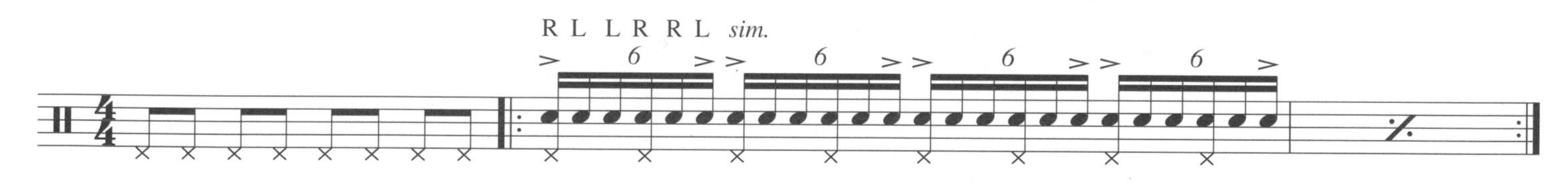

And at faster tempos, reduce the hat to quarters:

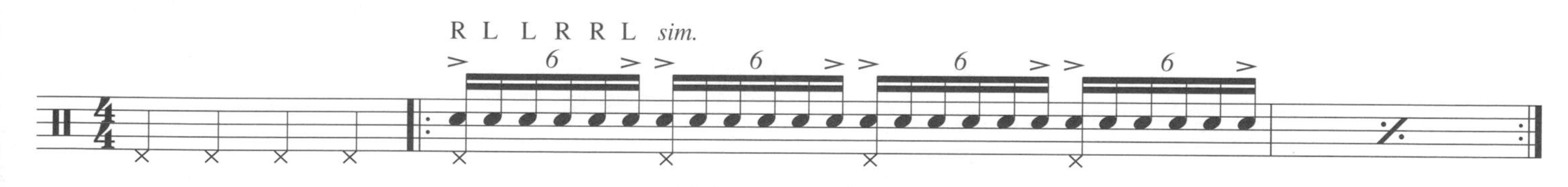

The best way to learn rolls is to start with double strokes. Build up your strength, speed, and confidence using double strokes so that you're comfortable bouncing your sticks more than just once at a time as you do with single strokes. As you transition into playing accents for the six-stroke roll, the awareness you'll acquire is that you're playing what I call "over the top" of the rolls, by counting the accents and knowing instinctively that the double strokes in between are being played automatically. Focus on hearing each stroke, and keep your rolls clean and defined.

To aid you in more quickly developing necessary strength and power, begin working on these exercises using your heavy practice sticks on your practice pad. After you're proficient on the practice pad with heavy sticks, move it over to the drumset using your regular drumsticks. In each setting, start off with a manageable bpm and increase your speed gradually. And always remember to relax!

Note: The preparation examples are played with an eighth-note swing (or shuffle). Listen to the video to get the feel for it. These preparation examples are essentially dropping out the double strokes, in order to make it easy to first get the right feel for the accents. Then we add in the double strokes, creating the six-stroke roll.

Hand Exercise 18a: Six-Stroke Roll with Moving Accents

Hand Exercise 18b: Single Sticking Accent Pattern with Toms

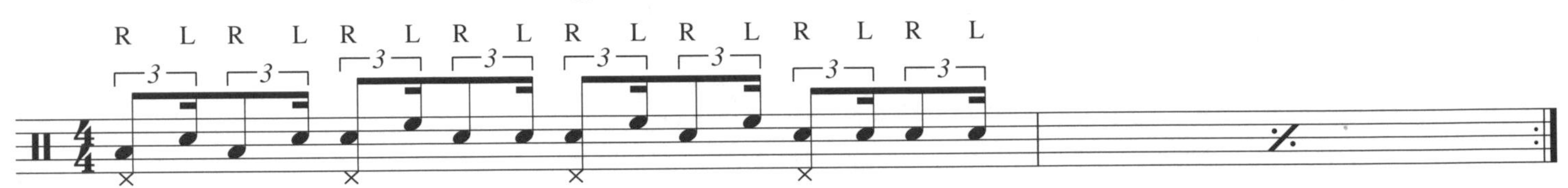

Hand Exercise 18c: Six-Stroke Roll Around the Kit

FEET

Now we are ready to increase your bass drum speed, build consistency, and learn to play cleaner and with greater control by applying many of the same principles we just applied to the hands.

Using Your Metronome to Chart Progress

I must again stress that the use of a metronome is vital to your progress as a drummer! A metronome helps you deliver a solid tempo in any situation you encounter, whether practice, rehearsal, recording, or playing live. And it is an essential practice tool. For example, suppose you decide to set your sights on playing double bass sixteenth notes at 200 bpm. Where do you start? How should you approach this?

Begin by just playing that double bass groove at whatever tempo is comfortable for you, without a metronome going at all. Then turn on your metronome and determine what that tempo happens to be. Next, make a chart to keep track of your progress. Write down the date and your beginning tempo. Now play along with the metronome at this speed continuously. Don't be discouraged if you cannot maintain this speed over long periods. This is to be expected. In fact, you may find that you actually need to *decrease* your bmp in order to maintain a consistent tempo. Be sure to chart that as well. Don't worry; you will certainly be able to sustain greater endurance after more practice at this specifically.

Now set metronome benchmarks so you create shorter-term goals, which act as a bridge toward your ultimate longer-term goal. So if your starting tempo happened to be 120 bpm and you want to eventually get to 200 bpm, set benchmarks at 130 bpm, 140 bpm, and so on, all the way up to your ultimate goal of 200 bpm. Some will be easier and faster to reach than others. This is completely normal.

Be patient with yourself as you progress toward your next benchmark. Spend the time and do the work to really master each benchmark. Don't be too quick to jump to the next one. You want to be able to play each bpm *comfortably*. Remember that you are building muscle, strength, and stamina as you journey toward your goal. And most importantly, you're building muscle memory. Your future self will thank you for achieving a level of comfort with each intermediate tempo, because within songs and drum fills, you will undoubtedly have opportunities to use double bass at each of the benchmark tempos you learned and mastered. And you want control at each of these different tempos, not just speed. When you put in this kind of work, your muscle memory will take over at any tempo and you'll be able to roll through any fill or song with ease because of your preparation and investment in quality.

PREPARATION VIDEO I

Use Ankle Weights

Use a pair of ankle weights during practice to help you build muscle faster as you move through each mechanic that follows. Similar to lifting weights when training for a sport, ankle weights will help increase strength and stamina for drumming. The stronger you are, the more you can relax as you execute these motions and therefore, the faster you will be able to play. I use five-pound ankle weights. You can find these in the fitness section of any department store or sporting goods store, or online.

PREPARATION VIDEO J

Bass Drum Technique

There are many different methods and theories regarding bass drum technique. Heel up, heel down, pivoting back and forth on the pedal, fluttering the feet on the pedals, etc. I've tried many of these techniques over the years and found that "heel up" works best for me. If you want to look into it further, a quick online search will provide plenty of interpretations of the differing bass drum techniques and their pros and cons.

Here is a brief summary of my technique.

- Sit up straight, with a flat back.
- Place your feet on the pedals so that they are under your knees for support. Your knees should be bent at 90 degrees, right angles.
- Make sure your feet are in line with your knees so they track properly; don't bow your legs out.
- Your bass drum stroke is generated initially from your hip flexor, then travels down through your quads and presses down. In a fluid motion, the end of your pedal stroke should be your calf muscle engaging and providing a "whipping motion" for your ankle to snap down to the pedal and slap the beater against the bass drum head.
- Relax your muscles and allow the pedal stroke to start at your body and travel down your leg to the pedal itself. Feel that whipping motion as you slap the beater into the bass drum head. Your muscles must be relaxed to allow this motion to be fluid.

Watch me demonstrate this motion on the video. Just as I mentioned before with the hands, I believe that if a given technique works for you, you'll perfect it in practice by making the necessary adjustments in order that your technique will adapt and fit into your playing style. Feel free to adapt it so it feels right for you. As long as you are relaxed and not feeling pain anywhere, you are on the right track.

Bass Drum Mechanics

The first mechanic is the one I use at the beginning of my warm-up. Always use a metronome. On the video I demonstrate each example at four speeds to give you some idea of how this looks and sounds at widely varying tempos. You should always begin slowly, at a manageable tempo, and then increase by 10 bpm at a time once you are feeling comfortable and proficient at each tempo. Feel the muscles working and remember to relax, especially at higher speeds.

When you reach a tempo at which you feel you must force it, back off a few bpm until you can regain that relaxed feeling. Then increase the tempo, maintaining that feel. This is a good one to do wearing ankle weights.

Bass Drum Exercise 19: Single Foot, Right

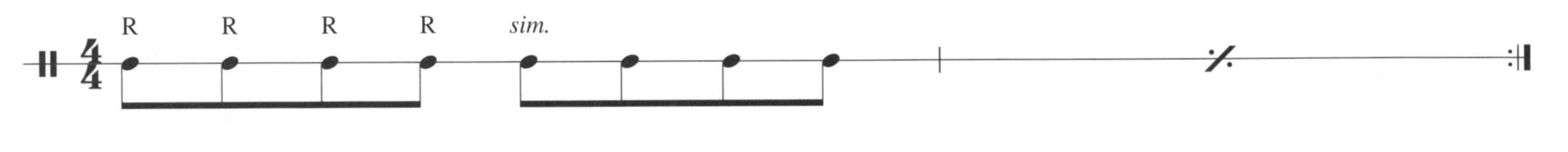

Bass Drum Exercise 20: Single Foot, Left

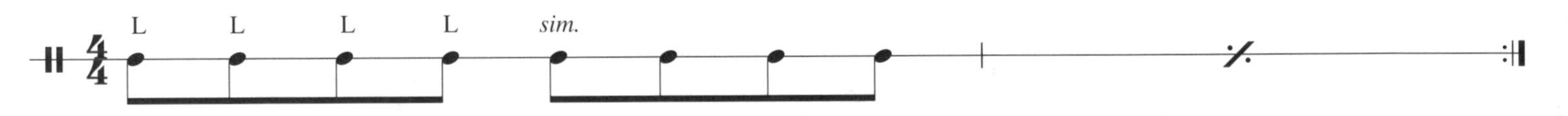

The next mechanic alternates feet every eight pedal strokes, or every measure. This is another good one to do while wearing ankle weights. It's an excellent mechanic for building strength, agility, and speed.

Bass Drum Exercise 21: Alternating Every Measure

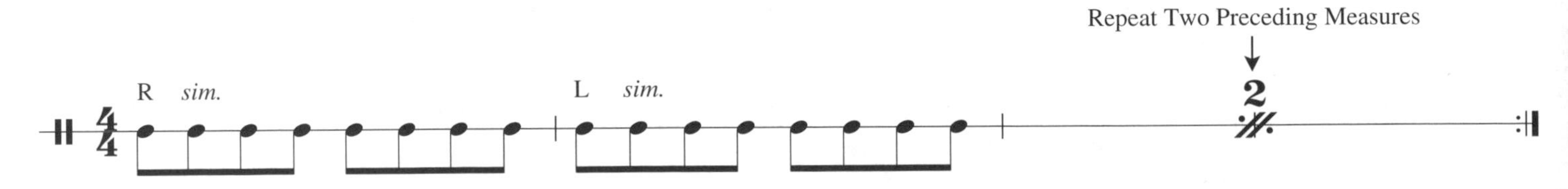

Let's bring it in a little tighter and alternate every four pedal strokes, still building strength and dexterity.

Bass Drum Exercise 22: Alternating Every Four Strokes

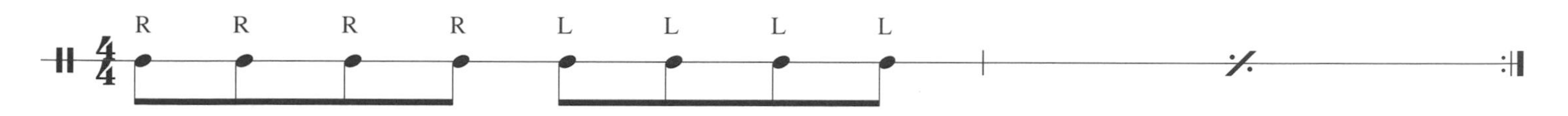

Alternating every stroke is a mechanic I use in my playing every day. Use ankle weights to build strength, and be thinking about how you can use this in your playing. Also, remember that you are creating a rhythm here, so feel the groove as you play through this. Start off at a manageable bpm and increase gradually. It's very important you relax. This mechanic provides the basis for most double bass drumming.

Bass Drum Exercise 23: Alternating Every Stroke

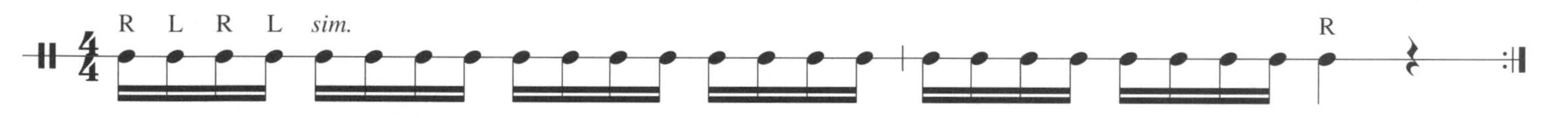

Exercises with Pauses

This next mechanic will help you build agility into your bass drum strokes. If you've built your strength up throughout the previous exercises, the ankle weights are optional for the remaining bass drum exercises. I recommend you do this one both as double bass, and to increase your single bass drum speed. Because we're stopping and starting, the purpose of this exercise is to go from 0 bpm to X bpm and stop in the cleanest possible way. Make your stops and starts crisp and on time as you focus on beginning and ending right on the beat. Be careful not to tense up on this one; let your bass drum strokes flow instead of trying to control the stops and starts.

Bass Drum Exercise 24: Alternating with Pauses

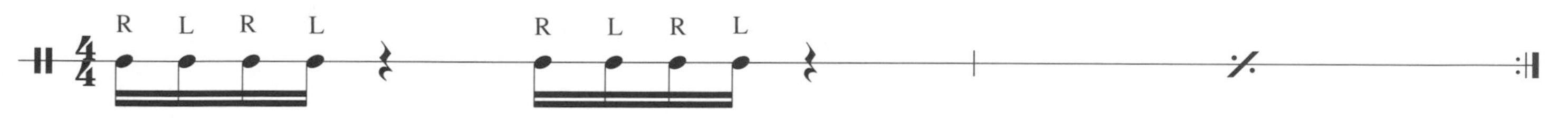

Patterns of Five

Let's continue working on agility, while thinking about how you might use your newfound speed and skills. The following mechanic has several applications, from being a bass drum fill or a song break, to providing a foundation for a groove. This is something that has made a huge impact on my playing, and this pattern of five can be moved around the beat to create interesting moments in music. The idea here is to flow, while keeping your stops and starts as clean as possible.

EXAMPLE VIDEO 25

Bass Drum Exercise 25: Patterns of Five

This next mechanic is what I call my "secret weapon" because it incorporates something that most drummers neglect in double bass drumming. It's easy to miss an opportunity to "roll into the One" when playing music. What I mean is that it's commonplace to hit a single kick on the One in any given song; that's what pretty much everyone does. But what if you anticipate that One and do something on the bass drum that rolls right into it? In most cases, you'll create a very cool effect that has a unique feel to it. Check out this mechanic and imagine how you can use it in your playing.

EXAMPLE VIDEO 26

Bass Drum Exercise 26: Patterns of Five Ending on 1 and 3

Endurance Runs with Accents

Now let's extend these double bass runs to build our endurance. Remember, it's not about how fast you can play; it's about how well you can play fast. And what that really means is being able to control both your velocity (how hard you are hitting) and your timing, keeping it even at any speed. A great exercise to develop better velocity control is to practice putting accents at key points, because in making the accent, you naturally must keep the rest of the hits at a lesser volume. And that is velocity control. So let's do an extended double bass run, accenting beat 1 of every second measure.

EXAMPLE VIDEO 27

Bass Drum Exercise 27: Extended Double Bass with Accents

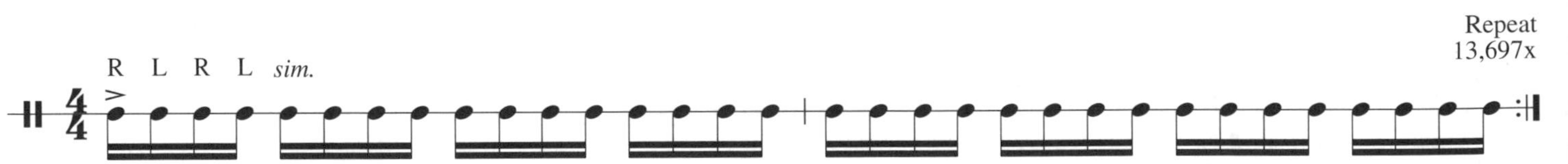

As you work through your bass drum mechanics, listen to the sounds you're creating and think about how you can use your new skills in songs and solos. When you start to bring everything together between your hands and feet, you should focus on developing your own sound and style. Some drummers fall into the trap of emulating their favorite artists to the point where they sound exactly like those artists. There's a big difference between being influenced by a drummer, and attempting to sound like them. It's important to play like *you*. Be yourself on the drums, and allow *your* personality to shine through. That's where the magic happens!

PART TWO

COMBINING HANDS AND FEET

In this section, you will begin to pull everything together between your skill on the snare and toms, and your newfound bass drum speed. As you play through these mechanics, you'll start to hear more of a musical quality emerge in your playing. Listen for that and pay attention to it as you make these mechanics a part of your drumming repertoire.

It's also important to know that these mechanics are notated with the right hand and right foot leading, but you can lead with whichever hand or foot suits your playing. What's important is that you execute each of the hits in the exercises provided. If you feel more comfortable leading double bass chops with your left foot, so be it. If that helps you play faster and cleaner, then that's what you should do.

 **PREPARATION VIDEO K**

BUILDING YOUR "CHOPS" LIBRARY

If you think of music as a language, it's important that your vocabulary be as broad as possible to give you the fullest possible range of expression. Whether you are writing, recording, or performing live, you will have a deep reservoir of ideas from which you can draw upon creatively. The concept of having a *chop library* in your head (and perhaps also written down if that helps you) is a great idea, because you can keep the music fresh and not worry about playing the same beats and fills too repetitively. Most drummers have their "go to" licks that they know they can use to light up a song or a venue. The question is, however, after that, "Now what?" Once you've played your big chop, where do you go from there? But if you build a larger personal catalog of drum chops, you will always have a new place to go! This is what we want.

Your chops can be simple or complex; from Charley Watts to Neil Peart. When I'm playing for an artist, most of my fills will be one beat, maybe two. If you're playing a "sideman" gig, your job is to *not* stand out, unless the artist calls for it. In those cases, your fills will be limited to something on the fourth beat, maybe just a snare hit with a cymbal crash, or single hit on the floor tom. If you're playing a gig as more of a hired gun, and the artist wants you to jump out a little bit, you can stretch your fills and chops to add more to that show or recording.

A few years ago, I was flying out to play a show with one of my best friends, Eric Grossman. Eric is an amazing bassist and has played all over the world with the band K's Choice. We were talking about the things great musicians do. What Eric said has always stuck with me: "You should be able to justify every fill you play." In other words, if the band stops after you play a drum fill and asks why you did it, what significance it has in the song, etc., you should be able to answer with confidence and clarity. If it fits, there is a reason.

Through the use of speed mechanics, your fills will be well rehearsed, drawing on established muscle memory, and controlled in timing and tone. This in turn allows you to really listen to the music, flowing with the energy of the song, and therefore to be *intentional* about what you are playing. You will find that it is this intentionality, this purposefulness, that will make your drumming "fit" each situation perfectly.

USE A METRONOME

Did I mention that already? *Continue* using a metronome for all these mechanics, because you know that this is vital to your progress as a drummer!

As you shift between your hands and feet in a drum fill, maintaining solid tempo is extremely difficult to do at first. Be sure to put in the time and attention needed to get those transition points even and smooth. You must coordinate and time your upper and lower limbs precisely together and that will take a little focused effort. Don't be discouraged if your playing sounds uneven or clumsy at first; you will be able to play fluidly after some practice. *The important thing is to keep playing.* After you get the hang of it, you'll find that you may actually be able to play faster using both your hands and feet than using *just* your hands or *just* your feet. But remember, it's not just speed we are after, but control. Don't sacrifice one for the other. We want smooth control at *all* tempos.

Remember, your metronome is the tool you are using to help you set benchmarks and measure your progress along the way. Be sure to chart your progress! And be patient with yourself. Spend the time and do the work to master each mechanic. Don't be too impatient to jump to the next exercise. You want to be able to play at a high bpm *comfortably* and that requires you to build strength, stamina, and muscle memory. Also, as I mentioned before, your future self will thank you for achieving a good level of comfort with each intermediate tempo, because within songs and drum fills, you will encounter opportunities to use all these mechanics at each of the tempos you mastered.

As a result of the work you're putting in *today*, your muscle memory will be able to take over at any tempo and you'll be able to play anything in your "chop library" at will.

WHEN TO MOVE ON, WHEN TO COME BACK

One more word about repetitive practice: As you repeat an exercise with proper focus, of course you will improve your accuracy, control, and fluency. However, after a certain point, you will find that your accuracy may begin to actually *deteriorate* slightly and errors begin to start cropping up *more often* and not less. This is normal. As neural motor control pathways tire, mistakes begin to happen. At that point, what you need is a short rest. But keep in mind that what needs to be "rested" is that very specific coordination pattern you have been hammering on.

To achieve this short "rest," you can often simply change the tempo (faster or slower). That may be enough to make it feel different to your muscle memory patterns and therefore cast it in a new "light." The same exercise at a significantly different tempo, in fact, is a slightly different action, to some degree, physically.

For a more significant rest, change to a different type of practice entirely, such as beginning to work on a completely different set of mechanics. If you had been working on six-stroke rolls, for example, try changing to double strokes, or for an even better "rest" of the upper body, change to work on some bass drum control mechanics. Another form of "rest" would be to perhaps stop playing drills altogether for a few minutes and just play along with music for a song or two, to revive your flow. After a few minutes of this changed focus, *then* come back to that same drill you were working on previously in which you first noticed the errors starting to crop up. Effective practice has a lot to do with watching yourself like this, and noticing your body's feedback and your results. Even as you remain focused on progress, be flexible. Practice itself is an art.

LINEAR HANDS AND FEET MECHANICS

 **PREPARATION VIDEO L**

Quads

Our first mechanic is widely known among drummers and is fairly simple. When executed properly, it creates an epic moment within a song. Think of the prominent fill that Neil Peart does in the Rush song, "Tom Sawyer." This mechanic is commonly known as a Quad because it incorporates all four limbs. It involves two hits with the hands, followed by two hits with the feet. Quads can be performed very fast, because the hands and feet each do only one hit and have three rest hits to "reload"—that is, to become ready for that limb's next hit.

This is also known as a *linear fill*, because nothing else hits at the same time. Linear grooves and fills are very popular and can be simple or complex. Linear grooves fit nicely into songs without sounding repetitive, since each limb is hitting something different. In other words, you can play sixteenth notes without hitting the same drum or cymbal twice. You can move them easily around the kit or use accents to add a groove feel to them. I will demonstrate this on the video for the examples that follow.

The example here has the quads being played between the snare and bass drum, but they're probably best known for being played between the floor tom, rack tom, and bass drum to give that "rumble" effect.

> True story: The way I learned how to play quads was, of course, practice. However, I was practicing them slowly and becoming increasingly frustrated. Every time I would start speeding up, I would make a mistake and have to start over. I had not yet learned how to practice with a metronome, so I kept getting ahead of myself. It was as if I was always stumbling forward; the momentum kept building to the point a mistake was made, and then I would fall down and the exercise would have to begin again. As it turned out, I just kept hitting "hand, hand, foot, foot; hand, hand, foot, foot" in frustration every time I messed up. Then suddenly I realized I was *doing it*! I just had to put my frustrated "hand, hand, foot, foot" combinations together and *poof*, it clicked and I was doing quads! Sometimes how you think of it is a big part of the problem, or the solution. The little "glitches" due to lack of attention can cause stumbling points, and we need to keep trying different ways of repetition until it "clicks." This was a happy accident, to be sure; however, it was not quite the smoothest ride getting there. If I had just used a metronome, I could have paced myself and learned to play quads with a gradual learning curve that built on a solid foundation.

EXAMPLE VIDEO 28

Hands and Feet Exercise 28a: Quads, Variation 1

And here they are shown with a quarter-note triplet feel. That is, if you view each quad set as a single event, or "note," for a moment, you would see three sets (three "notes") evenly spaced in two beats—which is a quarter-note triplet. Listen to this on the video and maybe execute that triplet rhythm first with stick clicks if necessary to first set up the triplet feel.

Hands and Feet Exercise 28b: Quads, Variation 1—Quarter-Note Triplet Feel

Quad Variations

The next mechanic is where things begin to get musical. You are now bringing your hands and feet together to bridge the gap and play odd groupings within each bar of music. Your hands are doing two, two, then six, while your feet fill the rest of the space in groups of two. Feel the groove as you play this, as it has a very natural movement to it.

Start off at a moderate tempo. This will help make it easier to understand what's happening here and catch the groove. Playing it too slowly will actually make it sound more complex and confusing. This is one of my all-time favorites in my "chop library." It is written here to be played with the snare and bass drum, but it sounds nicely melodic when you move it around the kit.

Once you're proficient with this mechanic, try starting on the snare drum, then moving to the rack tom and floor tom, then back again, alternating each time. Chances are, you'll figure out a new idea to use in your playing. Remember to relax, especially as you play faster. Keep your back flat and your posture in check.

Hands and Feet Exercise 29: Quads, Variation 2

Here is yet another way to build greater independence between your hands and feet. Groups of four on the hands act to turn the pattern around against the pulse, for an interesting rhythmic effect. This is a great one to practice over and over until you've built the muscle memory to the point where you can play it as a fill within a groove at pretty much any tempo. What you'll find is that you can use this mechanic all over the kit. Plus, it sounds really good when played fast!

Hands and Feet Exercise 30: Quads, Variation 3

This next mechanic is my favorite of the Hands and Feet combinations. It's the one I use at the end of my drum solo before going into the quads. It is fast and loud, and creates exciting moments in songs and drum solos alike. Just like the previous mechanic, this one sounds great when played really fast. But as it has its own groove to it, it also has a cool feel when played slower. When you play it on the rack tom and floor tom, it can sound like shoes tumbling around in a dryer!

It is critical to practice this mechanic with a metronome, because it can easily get away from you and cause you to lose the groove. If you are playing it slowly, you really have to make those hits count and stay in time with the pulse. Because it has its own rhythm to it, the other musicians can be thrown off easily, so you need to take charge when playing this as a fill and make sure you groove through it and come back in on "the One" nice and solid. When you do, it will create one of those "wow!" moments.

EXAMPLE VIDEO 31

Hands and Feet Exercise 31: Quads, Variation 4

And hands and feet exercise 31, moving around the kit:

The next mechanic is something you can use as a fill when you want a super-fast sextuplet feel. You play a set of four hits with your hands followed by two hits with your feet. Since you only have to worry about two quick strokes alternating with each hand, you can "reload" quickly, moving your hands into position and readying yourself to attack the next drum. And to make it even easier, you only have two hits on the bass drum in between. You can really let it fly with this one!

EXAMPLE VIDEO 32

Hands and Feet Exercise 32: Quads, Variation 5

And hands and feet exercise 32 with toms:

And remember, the quad mechanic can always be played as straight-ahead sixteenths, or with the triplet feel, as Neil Peart did in the "Tom Sawyer" example. Experiment with some variants of your own now.

NON-LINEAR HANDS AND FEET MECHANICS

PREPARATION VIDEO M

Hands over Feet

The next three mechanics in this section involve playing "hands over feet." In other words, you keep straight hits going on the bass drum *while* your hands play a pattern over this. Keeping the bass drums going underneath a drum fill creates a very powerful moment within a song. You can get really creative with this approach, and you will do a couple of exercises to get the basic idea. There are many possible variations that you'll figure out on your own as you master this technique. But it also requires a lot of precision and clean execution, or it will sound messy. The good news is that as you work on developing this precision here, this added level of control will positively impact *all* of your playing!

In this first mechanic, you are playing hands and feet in unison. Try this not only on the snare, as notated, but also on the toms and switching between snare and toms.

Hands and Feet Exercise 33: Hands over Feet, Variation 1

In the second mechanic below, you play "two over four": two hits with the hands, followed by two rests, as the feet play constant sixteenth notes. Relax as you play this and focus on the groove.

Hands and Feet Exercise 34: Hands over Feet, Variation 2

And the demonstration example moving this idea around the kit:

Below, we will continue with the solid bass drum sixteenths while playing four with the hands. Now you are *displacing* the rhythm in the hands so the second set of four sixteenths occurs 180 degrees opposite the pulse from the first instance. This creates an interesting accent feel.

EXAMPLE VIDEO 35

Hands and Feet Exercise 35: Hands over Feet, Variation 3

And the demonstration example moving around the kit:

PREPARATION VIDEO N

Making the Magic Happen

As you may have noticed throughout this book, I've encouraged you to be mindful of the tone, sound, and groove you create as a drummer. Now it's time to start bringing all those elements together and focus on what you create as a *musician*. Playing fast is actually fairly simple; you have the mechanics laid out and you practice them to build strength and speed. But playing fast with precision, tone, and groove is something entirely different. And beyond that, using all that control musically is something even bigger.

One of the biggest compliments on my drum solo is that people say it sounds "musical." What that means is I'm not just playing through a bunch of exercises and mechanics as fast as possible, but I'm creating music on a drumset. I use different tones, grooves, accents, and dynamics to build a musical quality that comes together through many hours of practice, trial and error, and constant focus on the overall sound I create.

The next examples offer some technique that will allow you to really start focusing on *making music*. There are infinite ways to make music and just as many interpretations of what music actually is. The goal here is to begin to feel it the way you imagine it should sound.

It's All in the Accents

Accents are an invaluable tool when creating a groove during a beat or fill. One common mistake drummers make when playing fast is they don't leave room for accents. They are playing so fast that they just don't think they have the time to wind up and smack an accent. The truth is, accents can actually help you play faster. Remember the six-stroke roll? The accents are used to help give you extra bounce, which allows you to play faster. Just try doing a six-stroke roll with no accents and you'll see what I mean.

One problem area for drummers who spend a lot of time on the practice pad is that they build up speed and strength, but forget that the ultimate goal is to take their skills to a drumset. When they sit down on an acoustic set, they may play as though they're still on the practice pad! So they may play fast, but it's not very musical. Using accents and dynamics and moving around the kit are easy to neglect on practice pads, especially if you practice on a single pad. But these elements are the essential step in bringing the drumset to life.

You can use single accents with one hand or both hands. You can use a single accent, or pepper them throughout the beat or fill you're playing. You can also use them at the beginning or end of a fill to create dynamics.

Let's look at some Speed Mechanics using accents and dynamics. This first one below is a commonly used accent pattern. It's a very simple, yet effective technique for creating a groove by breaking up the straight-ahead sixteenth notes.

One secret to using accents while playing fast is to "get up above it all," putting your focus primarily on the accents and making sure they're locked in with the metronome. The remaining notes simply fill in the space. But it's vital that you don't become complacent and focus solely on the accents while letting the in-between notes fall where they may. The notes that fill in the space must also be very intentional as they create the speed and movement between the accents. At times, you may even need to focus on these drum strokes more than the accents themselves. Try adjusting your attention between the accents themselves and the notes between as you repeat.

EXAMPLE VIDEO 36

Accent Exercise 36: Quarter-Note Accents on Hat

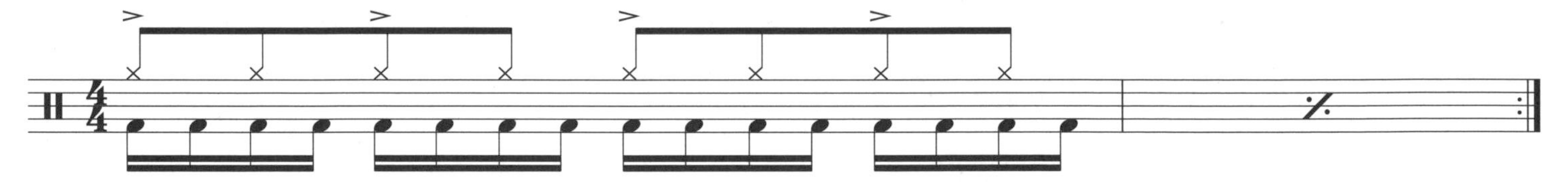

Another use of accents is to place two accents together. This creates a nice feel and a great sound, especially when you move the accents around.

EXAMPLE VIDEO 37

Accent Exercise 37: Two On, One Off

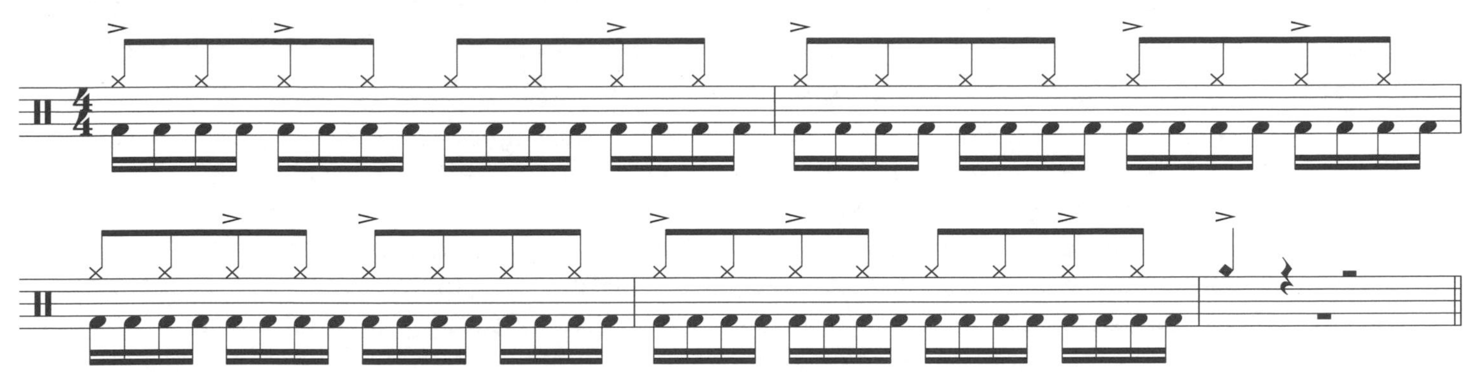

Using accents placed at random is commonplace in drum solos. You must practice this to have some idea as to where the accent placement works best for you.

EXAMPLE VIDEO 38

Accent Exercise 38: Random Accents

> For this example, notation of a specific pattern is contrary to the idea, which is to improvise random accent patterns. Simply watch the video and emulate this idea in an improvisational manner.

You can also move your accents around the kit, which adds complexity and texture to your fills. This is where drum and cymbal placement becomes important. As you move around the kit, be sure that the spacing of your toms and cymbals doesn't get in your way and slow you down. Also, this is where muscle memory comes into play. You can really let your hands fly around the kit while placing accents on the toms. You can do as many variations of this as you can make up. A creative way to use accents in a band situation is to have the band follow your accents, either in an instrumental break or leading into a verse, chorus, bridge, or guitar solo. You can become an invaluable member of any band when you introduce these kinds of musical gems that lift songs above the average structure of verse, pre-chorus, chorus, etc. The more musical you can make them, the more important you'll become as part of the songwriting process.

For this mechanic, be sure your accents are clean, along with the drum strokes between the accents. You can base the "in between" drum strokes on the snare drum, although you can base them on the floor tom or other toms as well.

Accent Exercise 39: Accents Around the Drumset

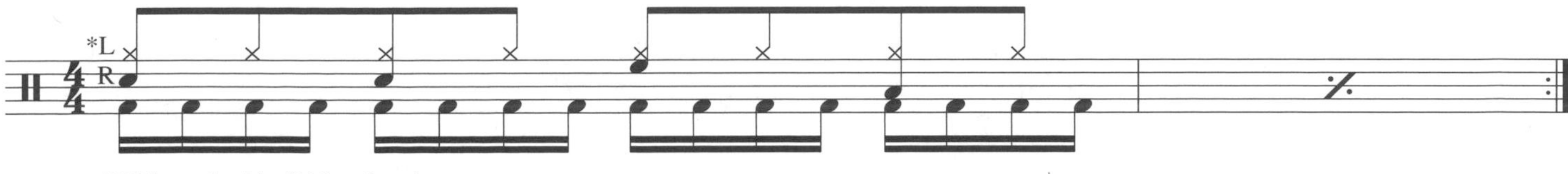

*With weak-side (L) hand on hat

Now try making up a few of your own accent patterns and move them around the kit. See what kind of interesting patterns you can create!

PREPARATION VIDEO O

Effectively Using Double Strokes

If you are playing rock or metal, you'll most likely be using single strokes exclusively. Because double strokes don't pack the same punch as single strokes, they tend to drop out in the mix. You may have seen a band live or on video in which the drummer plays a fast drum fill and you can't hear it. There can be several reasons for this, such as poor mic placement, bad mix, or poor drumming technique. This same effect can also occur when the drummer tries to use double strokes. Unless you can play double strokes at the same volume as single strokes, save your double strokes for the times they'll be most effective. If you're playing jazz, you will be able to use double strokes more often because jazz incorporates more finesse than power. However, there is always a place for double strokes, even in rock and metal. During intros, song breakdowns, and muted verses, double strokes can be a very effective tool for playing fast without dominating the mix.

A few years back, I played a show where a famous guitarist sat in on "Whole Lotta Love." During the breakdown, I started playing double strokes between the ride cymbal and hi-hat. The guitarist looked over at me and did a double take. He smiled and nodded in approval at what I was doing. When the song ended, he made it a point to come over and shake my hand before leaving the stage. After the show, he told me he had never seen or heard anyone play fast like that with so much power and definition; he was talking about my double-stroke work in the breakdown. Everything else I did in the song was single strokes, but it was the choice of double strokes, played at the right time, that made the real impact. He called me a "monster drummer." Of course, it was beyond flattering. I went to see his band play some months after that and they let me in for soundcheck. When he saw me from the stage he said, "Hi Monster!" and told everyone about my drumming. He's called me Monster ever since.

Here's an example of what I played. It's very simple, but effective, and sounds great at around 100 bpm.

EXAMPLE VIDEO 40

Drumset Exercise 40: Double Strokes Between Ride and Hi-Hat

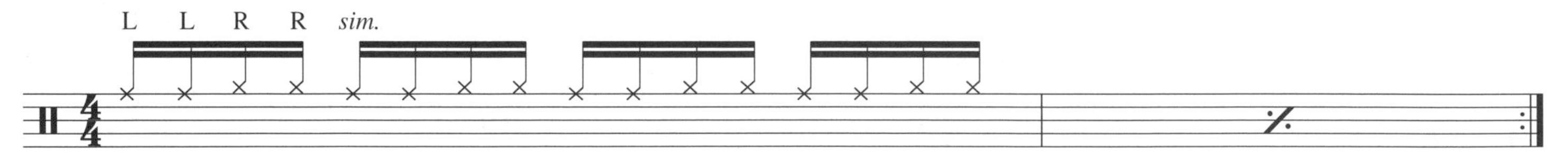

PREPARATION VIDEO P

The Blast Beat

There are several versions of the *blast beat* and just as many versions of the story about its origin. But a book titled *Speed Mechanics for Drums* would be remiss if we didn't cover at least a few of its variations and potential implementations.

The traditional blast beat is a single-stroke roll alternating between the snare drum and kick drum. The ride hand is usually playing in unison with the kick drum. Here is a notation of the traditional blast beat.

EXAMPLE VIDEO 41

Drumset Exercise 41: Traditional Blast Beat

EXAMPLE VIDEO 42

The Bomb Blast

The *bomb blast* is essentially a combination of blast beat and double bass drumming. When measured in sixteenth notes, a bomb blast has eighth notes on the snare played above a sixteenth-note kick pattern. Most drummers lead with the snare, whereas the traditional blast beat leads with the bass drum.

Drumset Exercise 42: Bomb Blast

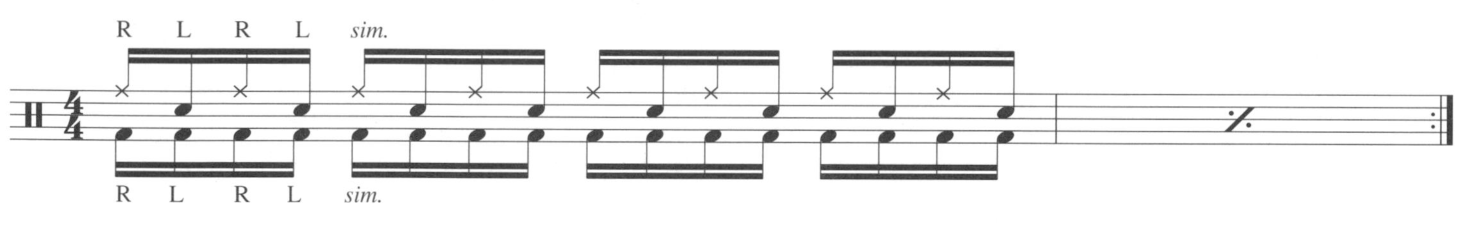

EXAMPLE VIDEO 43

The Hammer Blast

The *hammer blast* (also known as the *hyper blast*) is played with the snare and bass drum in unison. Instead of playing alternating eighth notes on the bass drum and snare, and thus creating a sixteenth-note roll, the hammer blast is played as straight eighth notes.

Drumset Exercise 43: The Hammer Blast

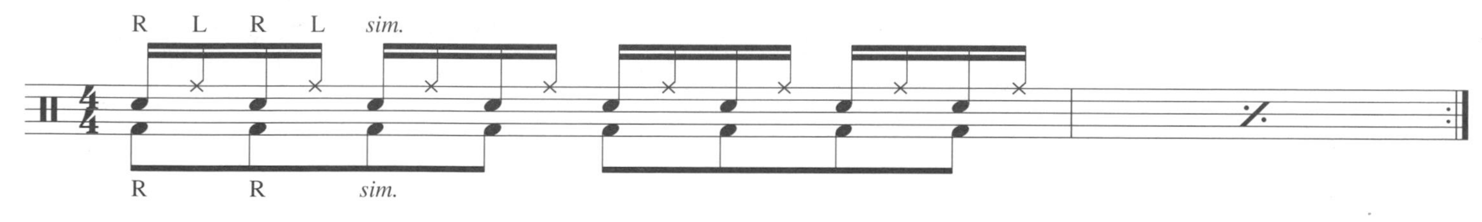

And with sixteenths on the kick:

The Triplet Blast

To be honest, I really don't do much with blast beats these days. They certainly have a place in music and are a valuable tool for the drummers who use them. I've gotten away from them because it's tough to groove while playing a blast beat. I do have one variation that I use as a drum fill or at the end of a build up. It is played in triplet form and consists of the hands playing the first stroke in unison, while the bass drum follows with the second and third stroke. I've played this as a beat in metal songs and it can be quite effective. In the song "Kaleidoscope" from the video that accompanies this book, you'll hear this triplet blast as we head into each of the breakdowns, as well as the finale of the song.

Drumset Exercise 44: Triplet Blast

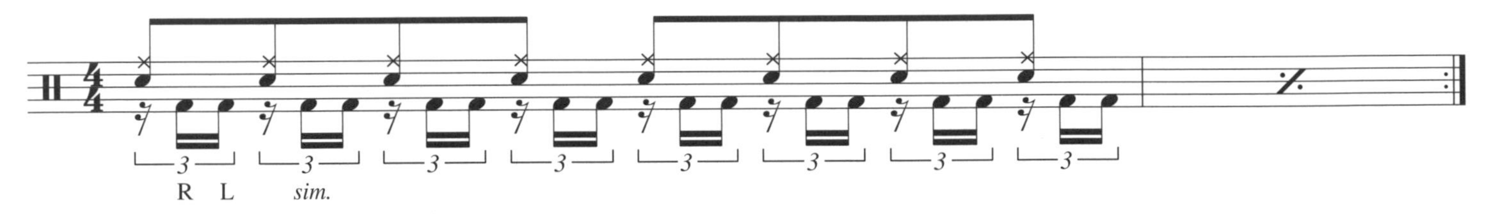

FILL APPROACHES

The following set of examples will present a broader set of fill options to use in different types of situations, as well as challenge you to implement the speed and control skills you have been developing. We will begin with fills on a single drum first, focusing on velocity control, and build from there.

Single Drum Fills

For exercise 45, use your strength to punch the fill hard but evenly and with control, so it will stand out well in the mix. Watch out for the natural tendency to tighten up at the higher tempos and allow your fills to become too quiet. Keep your power up.

Fill Exercise 45: Single Drum Sextuplets

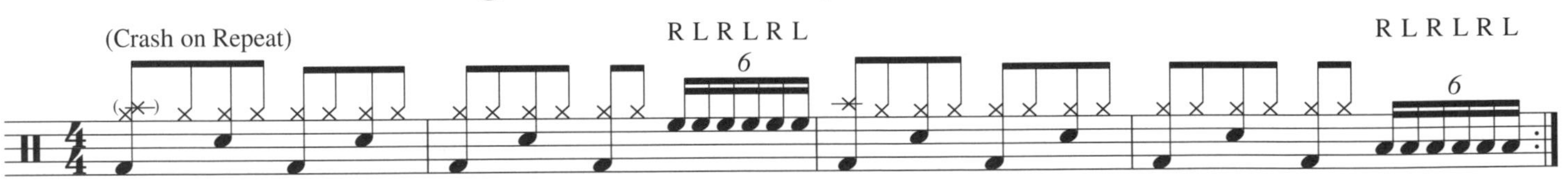

Altering the Momentum

Next let's try a fill that begins at a moderate rate and then doubles its speed at the end. Focus on keeping the same power level through the end of the fill, not allowing it to fade as you move into the cymbal crash on beat 1.

EXAMPLE VIDEO 46

Fill Exercise 46: Increasing Momentum

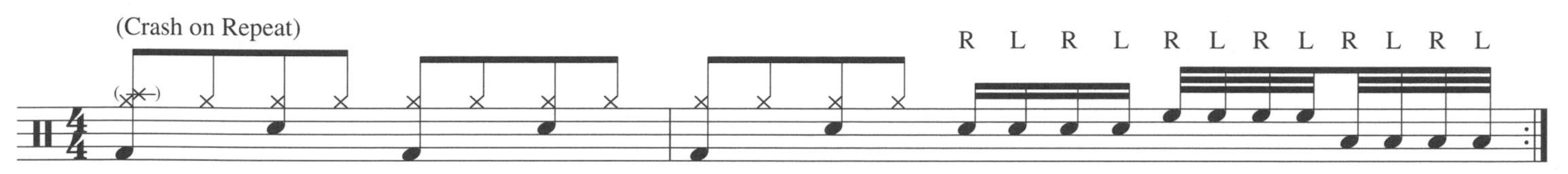

And now the opposite—begin the fill faster, then slow down.

EXAMPLE VIDEO 47

Fill Exercise 47: Decreasing Momentum

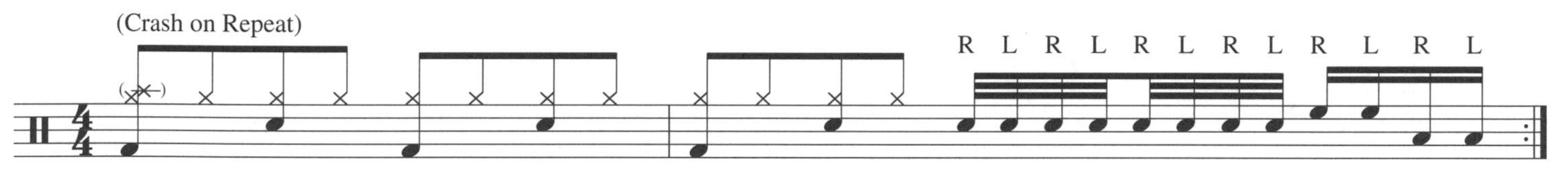

Sixteenths vs. Triplets

The following examples change the feel between even sixteenths and sixteenth-note triplets. Keep your pulse steady at every tempo and make the change seamless and fluent.

EXAMPLE VIDEO 48

Fill Exercise 48: Sixteenths into Triplets

EXAMPLE VIDEO 49

Fill Exercise 49: Triplets into Sixteenths

EXAMPLE VIDEO 50

Fill Exercise 50: Spicing It Up

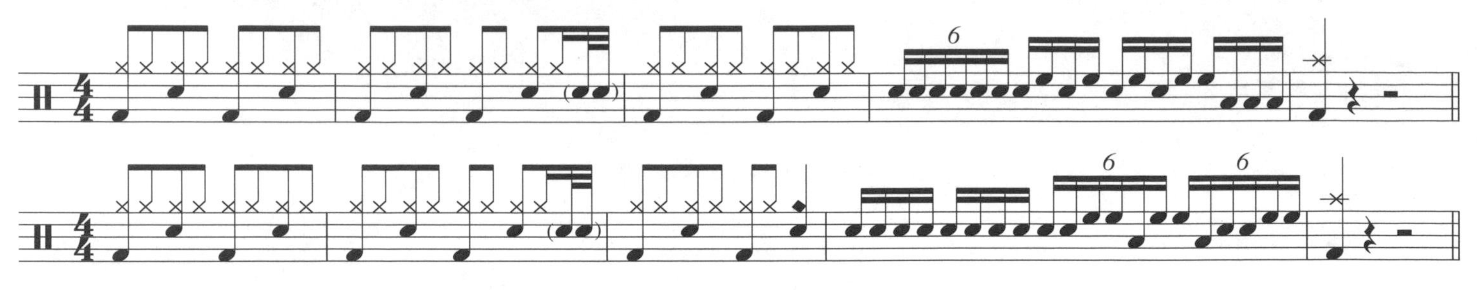

Hand and Foot Rhythmic Combinations

The following two-measure fill creates a natural emphasis first on downbeats (on 1, 2, 3), then switching to upbeats (on the &s of 4 and 1), then back to downbeats (on 3, 4).

EXAMPLE VIDEO 51

Fill Exercise 51: Hand and Foot Rhythmic Combinations

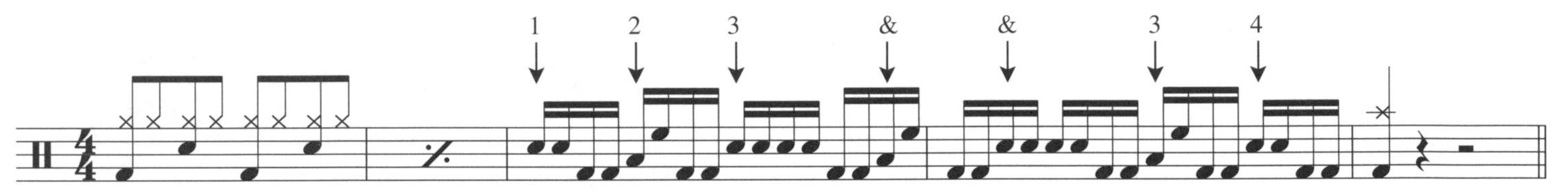

Next is a one-measure fill that begins with the bass drum and creates a natural accent feel on three consecutive upbeats (the &s of 1, 2, and 3).

EXAMPLE VIDEO 52

Fill Exercise 52: Consecutive Upbeats

Non-Linear Fills

Now let's add the bass drum into a straight sixteenth fill. Notice how a simple two-beat rhythmic pattern is first established, then altered to create a moment of rhythmic interest by delaying the floor tom, and finally the original rhythmic motif returns to complete the fill.

EXAMPLE VIDEO 53

Fill Exercise 53: Non-Linear Fill

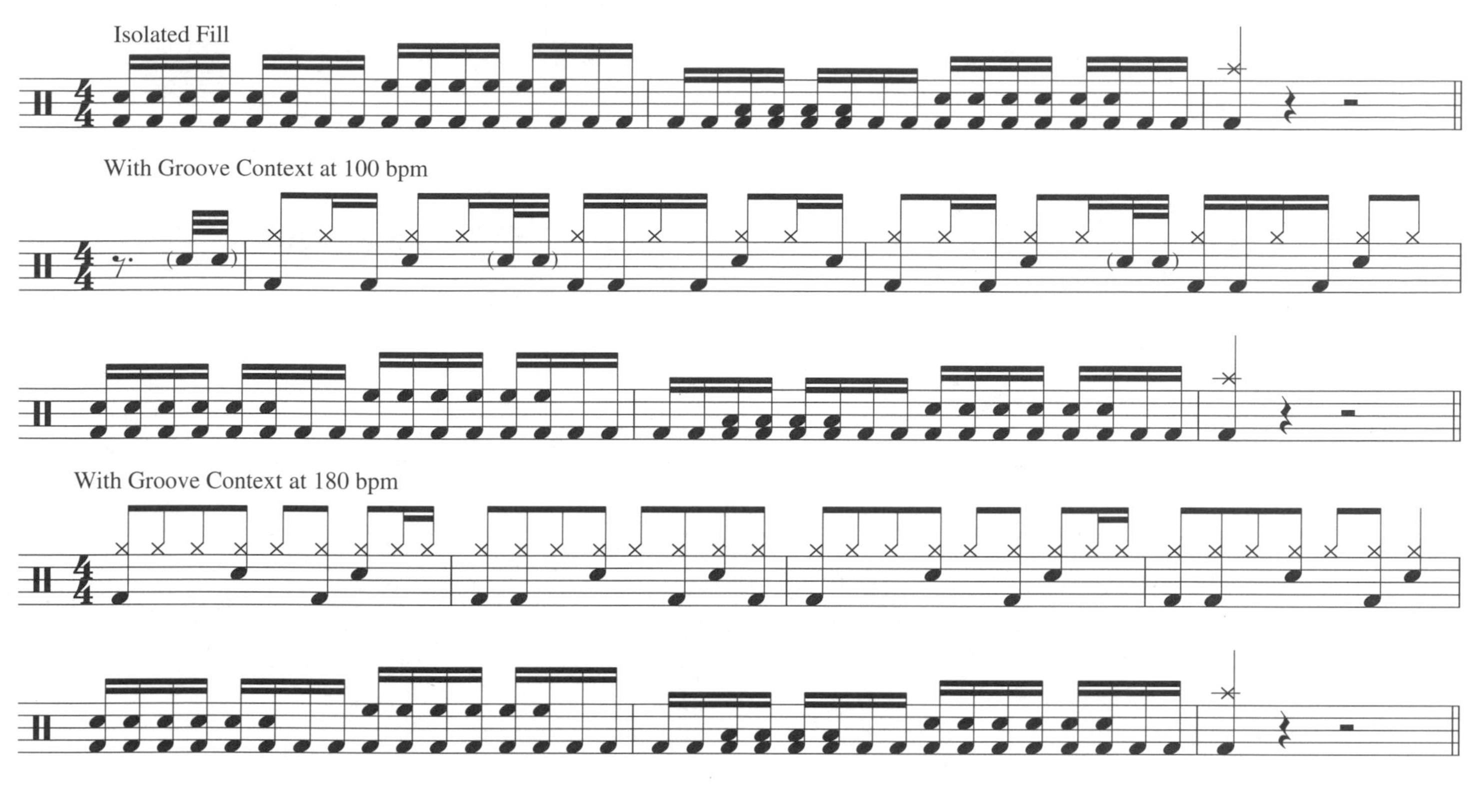

Altering Entrance and Exit Points

Fill exercise 54 begins the fill on the & of 1. This approach obscures the normal fill point just enough to catch the listener off guard, rather than being so obvious and predictable. And yet it smoothly rolls out to an easy completion.

EXAMPLE VIDEO 54

Fill Exercise 54: Delayed Starting Point

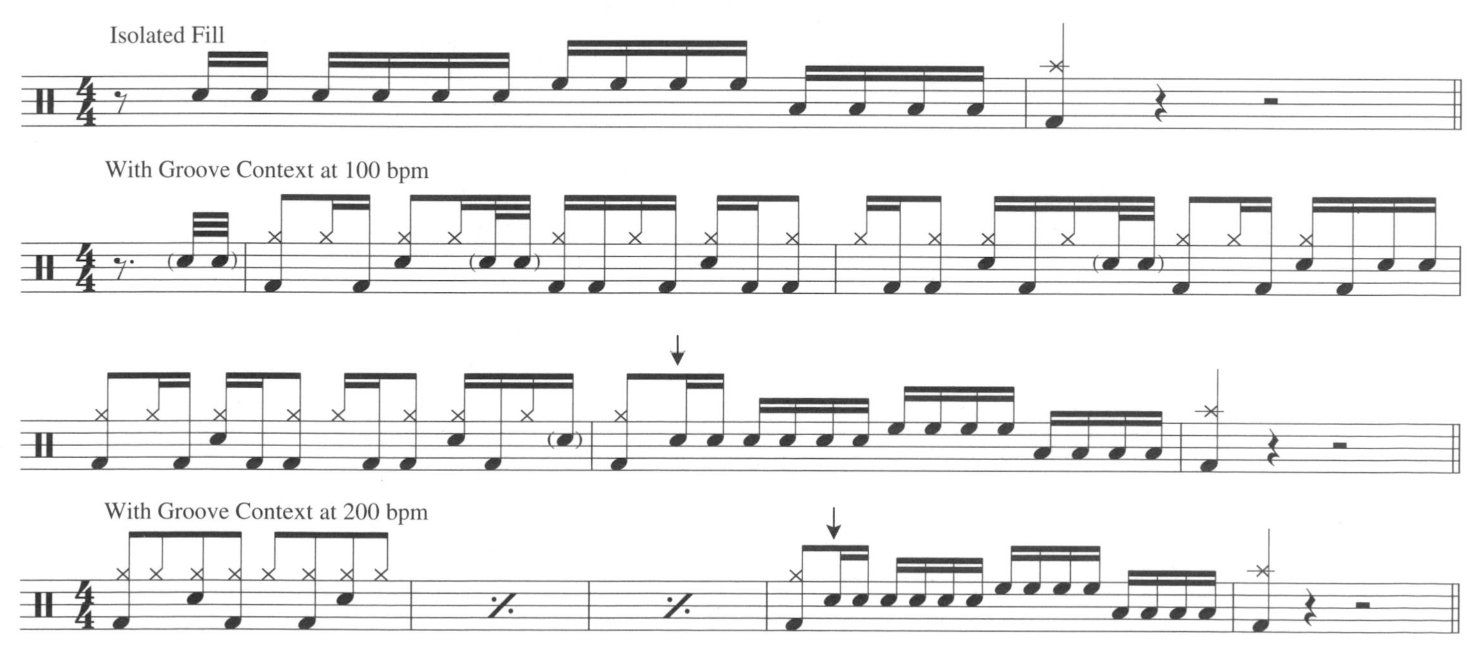

EXAMPLE VIDEO 55

Fill Exercise 55: Ending Early for a Dramatic Pause

Isolated Fill

With Groove Context at 100 bpm

With Groove Context at 200 bpm

PART THREE

PUTTING IT ALL TOGETHER

BALANCING SPEED AND GROOVE

There are many YouTube videos of drummers who can play super-fast blast beats, crazy-quick double bass, etc. Some are using bass drum pedals that strike the drum twice for each single hit, thus doubling the speed of their pedals. Some are great at high-speed drumming, but tend to fall apart when the song slows down and they need to play with style and feeling.

Remember this: Playing fast is merely one aspect of drumming. It is a tool you can use to create an exciting moment within a song, or create an exciting song in its entirety. It is impressive to see drummers play really fast and I have the utmost respect for them. If you're hoping to have a career in music, my best advice is to become as well-rounded as possible in all forms of drumming. Use speed as your secret weapon, but not your only weapon. The flip side of the coin is groove. When you watch those videos, listen to what the drummers are playing with their hands. They may be playing ultra fast with their feet, but do the hands sound stiff and robotic? Or does it feel human and organic? We don't want to simply emulate programmed drums with no groove, dynamics, or feeling. Remember, it's about the quality of the hits, not just the quantity.

CHOOSING YOUR MOMENTS TO SHINE

This is one of the most important things you can learn as a musician. Choosing when and how to jump out and make something happen in a song is an art form unto itself. It requires instinct, balance, and the ability to make your mark before diving back into the song. You need instinct to know the suitable drum lick and the appropriate moment to play it. You need to balance that drum fill or groove with the rest of the song—too much and it sounds out of place; too little and it won't leave much of an impression. Just as crucial is the ability to jump out and play your fill for that moment, then fall right back in step with the band. The smoother your transitions in and out, the more powerful the impact you will make.

I once sat in with a band in Japan. They were opening for my band and didn't speak a word of English. Their soundcheck was very impressive and I asked our tour manager if he could arrange for me to sit in with them. They were super excited and we figured out what song we would play together. When the time came, I got up on the drums and counted in the song. We were cruising along and I thought ahead to a place in the song where I could throw in a fill that would be totally unexpected. When the moment arrived, I launched into a pretty blistering quad fill and then slipped right back into the song as if nothing had happened. The guys in the band were stunned and looked at each other, then looked at me. I looked around as if to say, "What was that?" and we all cracked up. The singer actually started laughing and had to stop singing while the band kept playing. Needless to say, it was one of those magic moments. Instinct played a big part in knowing that the timing and fill I played would make quite a splash. If it had been a more serious situation, I would have throttled back and played a more subdued fill, especially at that point in the song. Thinking ahead to what *wants to happen* in the song is a big part of this craft. Instinct is acquired over time and cannot be taught. That's why I place so much emphasis on encouraging you to think about your playing as you're practicing through each of these exercises. Imagine how you'll use speed mechanics in your playing, and you'll begin to develop your instinct for playing what you want, when you want, for just the right impact in any situation you may encounter.

GROOVING WITH SPEED

If you've caught on that groove is a reoccurring theme in this book, you're right on track. Groove is what drives the song. The ability to lock in as a band and create movement is the foundation of the songs you play. Have you ever listened to a song and thought it was good, but something wasn't quite right? You like the lyrics, the guitar riff is cool, the vocal melody is solid, but there's just something holding the song back. If you listen to that song now with this in mind, you may realize that what's missing is the groove. The tempo may be fluctuating, or more often than not, the musicians are not locked into a groove together.

Same thing with speed mechanics: the ability to form a groove while playing at any speed is what helps give that magic *feel* to your playing. You may have people tell you they can't put their finger on it, but there's something special about the way you play. Chances are, you have a good groove. Being able to groove at high speed is a real talent that requires discipline.

FOCUS ON EACH LIMB

Think of your limbs as a band: each member of the band helps to form the groove. If the kick drum is providing the foundation, is it hitting right on the beat? Practice this with a metronome and record yourself. Listen to yourself play and isolate the kick drum. If it's not hitting right on the beat, you may need to make some adjustments and practice until you get the bass drum landing exactly where it needs to be. You may need to slow down to make this happen. Don't worry; you'll be forming good habits going forward.

Is your hi-hat hand grooving? Are you accenting just a bit to make that happen or are you plowing through with no dynamics? Slow down and play just the hi-hat in a way that has a musicality to it. If you do this, you will notice a vast improvement in the sound of your playing. Do the same thing on the ride cymbal. Make it groove, then play flat out and enjoy the difference in overall sound and vibe.

How about your snare hand? The snare drum is where you have a little more flexibility to help create your sound. Some drummers hit the snare right on the beat, while others are a little bit behind it. Experiment with this and see where you like hearing the snare drum land in your playing. You can even see a visual of this if you record your playing using a program like Pro Tools®, Logic®, or GarageBand®. On the screen you can see where your snare lands in reference to the beat. Don't worry if your snare hits don't land right on the beat; it may add a little swing to your playing and help to create your own signature groove. When you're not playing a beat that requires hitting the snare drum in rapid succession, you may find yourself lightly tapping the snare drum in between hits. These are called ghost notes and also help to form your groove. Ghost notes are their own discipline, but for our discussion here, just know that I encourage you to study them and use them.

ROLLING INTO THE ONE

In Part 2, there was a speed mechanic that I call my "secret weapon." For reference, it's Bass Drum Exercise 26: Patterns of Five Ending on 1 and 3. Now you can see how this fits into a beat and in different situations on the drumset. It is a way to "roll into" a bar of music, or several bars of music if you're using it as the foundation for a beat. It is four sixteenths followed by a beat that lands on the 1, hence the notion of "rolling into" a bar of music. You also can do them in rapid succession to create a drum fill on the bass drum. This mechanic can give you a very unique groove that most bands respond to favorably, usually with much enthusiasm!

EXAMPLE VIDEO 56

Drumset Exercise 56: Rolling into the One

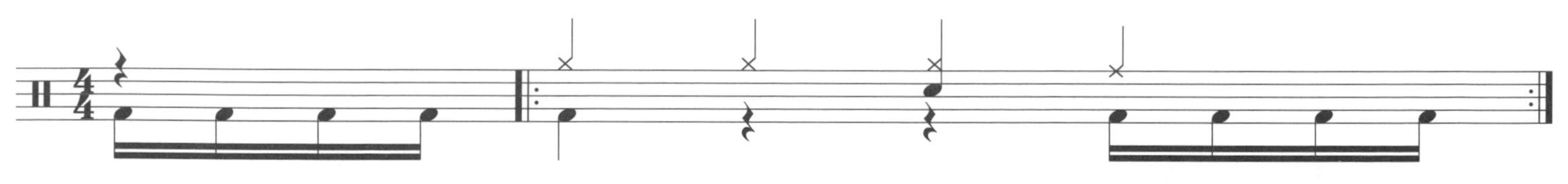

And here is the full transcribed demonstration example played on the video, showing how rolling into the one can be applied in context. Try covering this, then experiment with your own variations.

LONG DOUBLE BASS RUNS VS. SHORT BURSTS

There's no wrong answer here; it's all a matter of preference. It may also have to do with how much strength and stamina you have. Most importantly, it all comes down to the song. If the song you are playing calls for a long double bass run, go for it. If it would be more appropriate to play short bursts, go with that. Try both and let your band decide. Don't do something just because it's impressive; do it because it fits the song. Sounds cliché, but always play for the song. If what you're playing gets boring, write more songs that fit your new skill level!

Here are some speed mechanics that incorporate short bursts of speed. I encourage you to do as many variations of these as possible. Accenting a guitar riff, playing against it in the breaks, or maybe a little of both. Get creative with your double bass playing. This is where practice really pays off with your power, quickness, and precision.

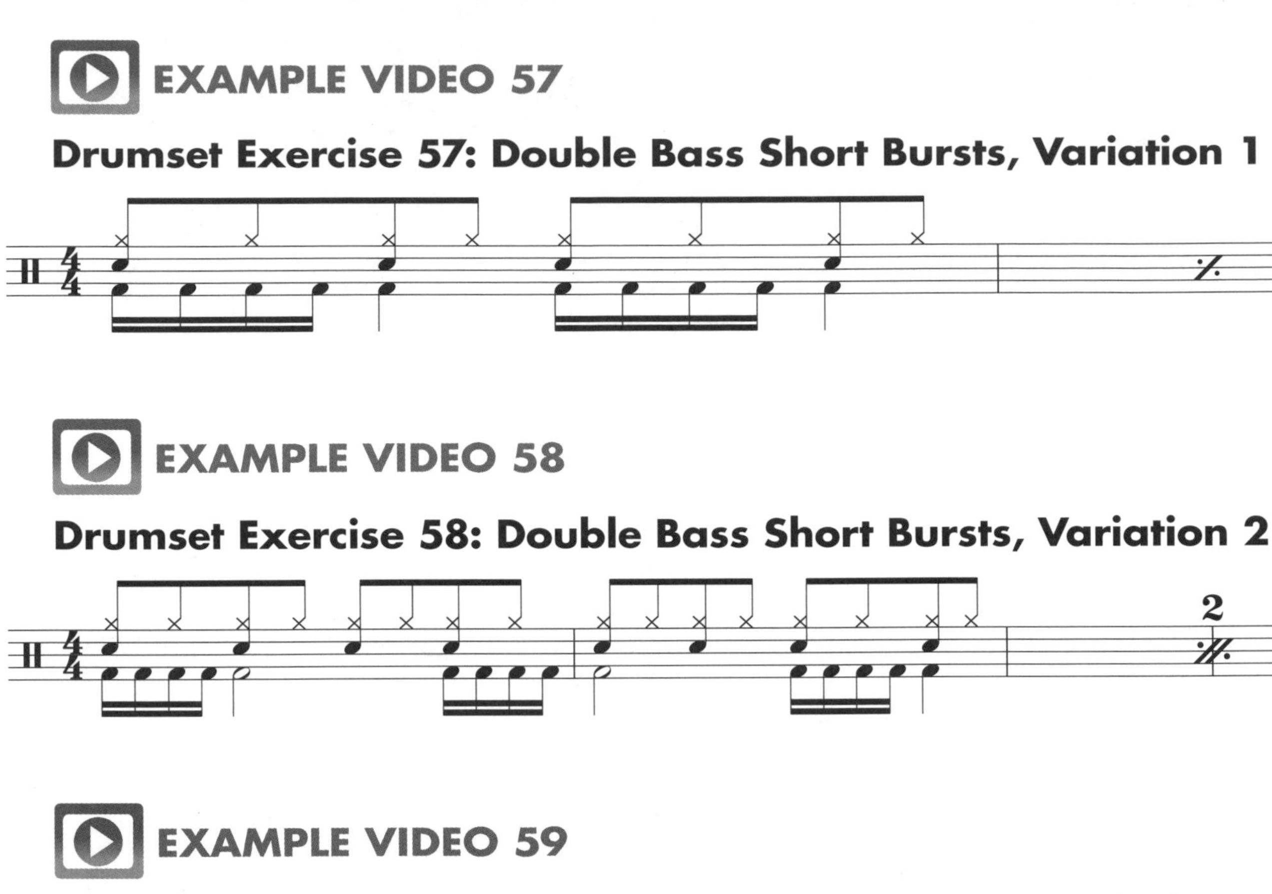

EXAMPLE VIDEO 57

Drumset Exercise 57: Double Bass Short Bursts, Variation 1

EXAMPLE VIDEO 58

Drumset Exercise 58: Double Bass Short Bursts, Variation 2

EXAMPLE VIDEO 59

Drumset Exercise 59: Double Bass Short Bursts, Variation 3

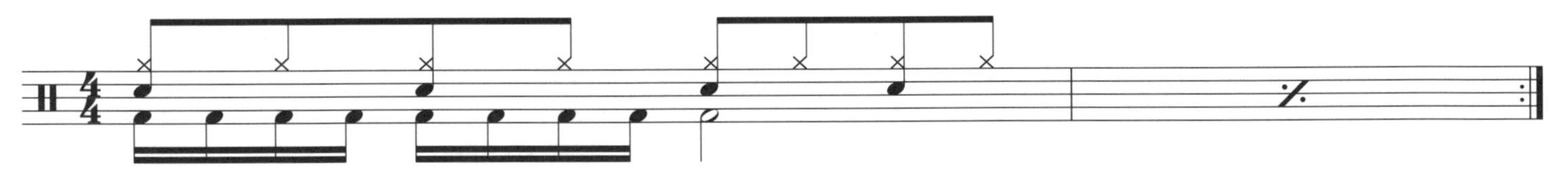

And the "Kaleidoscope" variation:

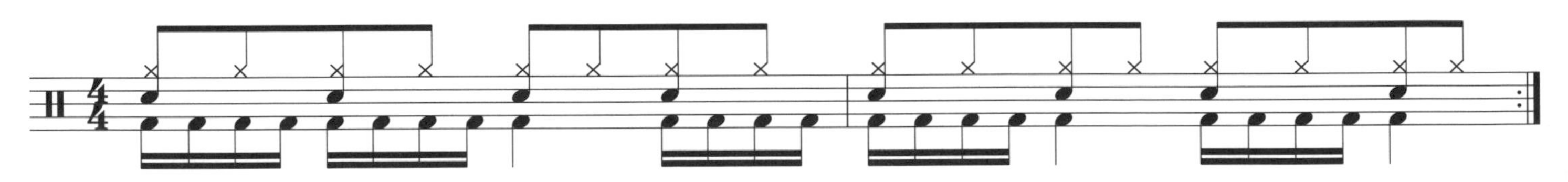

EXAMPLE VIDEO 60

Drumset Exercise 60: Double Bass Continuous Run with Downbeat Snares

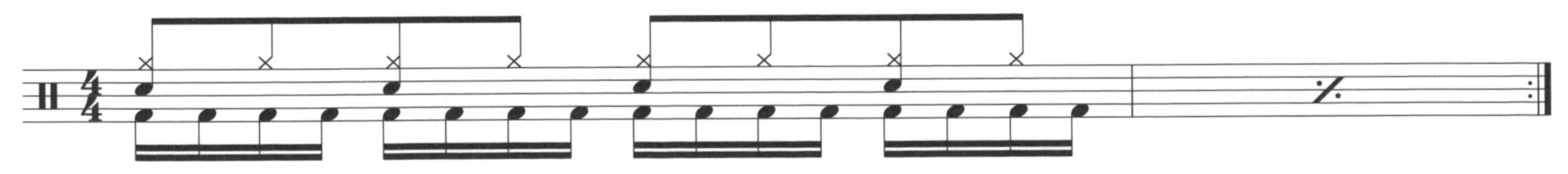

EXAMPLE VIDEO 61

Drumset Exercise 61: Double Bass Continuous Run with Upbeat Snares

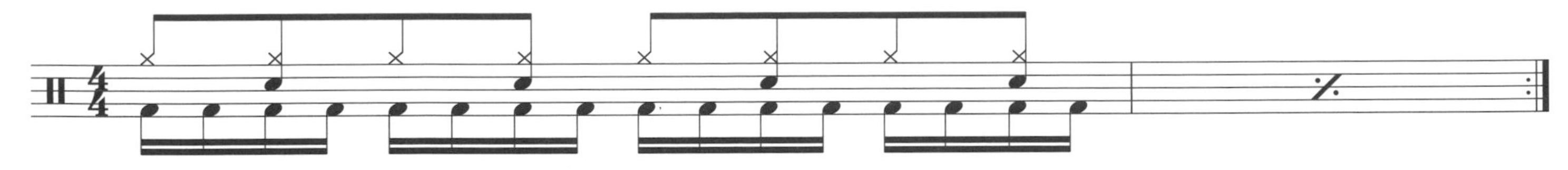

PREPARATION VIDEO Q

SOLO PIECES

When your band gives you a space to solo, it is your opportunity to show the audience who you are. The solo is *your* moment. Prepare yourself and make the most of it. Always have a plan, whether it be loosely structured or specifically written out. Even short solos are worth your utmost focus and attention. "Winging it" never compares to having something fully put together and ready to go. Launch into your solo without having to think about what you're going to play. If you do happen to improvise, at least you will have something to come back to in case what you're playing isn't working out. Playing with speed is all about confidence. You must lean into it, so to speak. The more prepared you are and the more confidence you have, the farther you can lean into it.

It's like public speaking. Public speaking is one of the biggest fears people have. Do you know why? Having done a lot of public speaking, I can tell you that the real fear is based in lack of preparation. The thought of being in front of an audience with nothing to say or forgetting what you were going to say is absolutely terrifying. If you had to speak to an audience about a topic you knew very little about, you'd either be scared or prepared. You'd hopefully take the time to study your topic and make it your goal to know more about it than anyone else in the room. If you had to speak to an audience about your day-to-day life, you'd most likely be comfortable because you're the expert. You can speak with full confidence because you know your topic better than anyone in the room.

Be the expert of your solo pieces. Know everything about them. Whether comprised of a short break in a song or a five-minute stretch where the band leaves the stage, your solos should be your most confident moments onstage. If they aren't, you need to practice them more. If you are fully prepared, you'll look forward to your solos. Having a basic idea of what you're going to do, then hoping for the best onstage is no match for having something prepared that you've been practicing for weeks or months. I've worked with many artists who have the expectation that they'll get onstage and the magic will take over, so they'll be fine. It makes you wonder how much better their performance would be if they just did the work and prepared themselves.

When you're soloing, envision it as a song unto itself, even if it's a short break—a couple of bars. Decide what you want to accomplish. If you can make it musical, so much the better. Maybe break it up into two parts or more. Begin with something rhythmic, then finish with a scorching quad run. Or maybe do the same thing in reverse: come out of the gate flying and end up with a tasteful exit on the snare. Whatever you choose to do, it is indeed your choice. Let your personality come through and make your mark. With regard to any solo opportunity, your objective should be to have the audience talking about it afterward!

In the third breakdown of the song "Kaleidoscope" on the video that accompanies this book, there are three solo piece/drum chops that I play. Here are each of those, notated as Drumset Exercises 62–64.

ADVANCED FILL CONCEPTS: PLAYING THROUGH BEAT ONE

EXAMPLE VIDEO 62

Drumset Exercise 62: Playing through Beat One

ADVANCED FILL CONCEPTS: COMPOUND RHYTHMS

EXAMPLE VIDEO 63

Drumset Exercise 63: Compound Rhythm 1

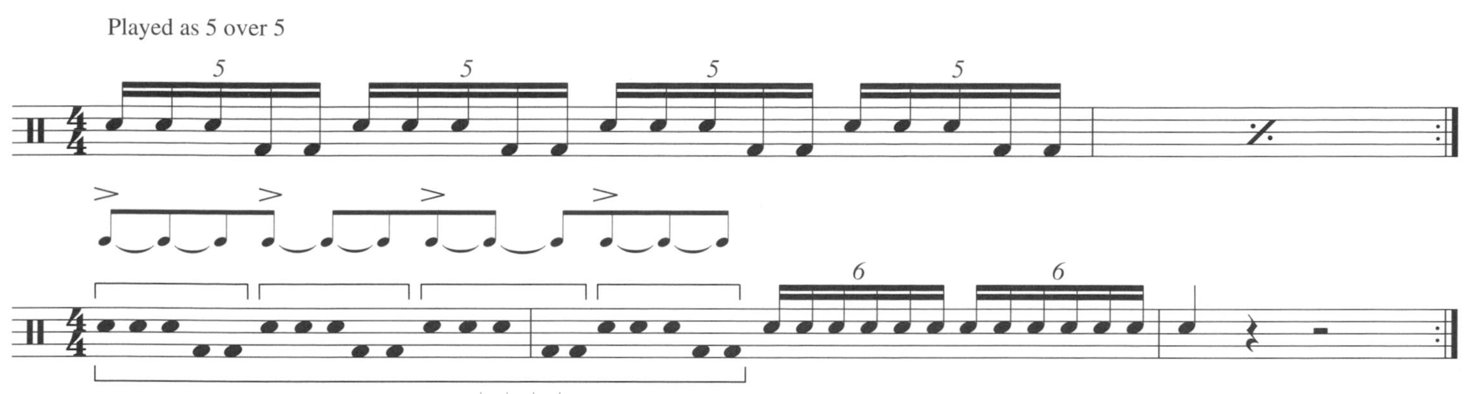

EXAMPLE VIDEO 64

Drumset Exercise 64: Compound Rhythm 2

Add double bass, but notice how the same simple accent rhythm on the snare still holds it all together.

ALLOW FOR BREATHING ROOM

The first time I saw Slayer, the word that came to mind was "unstoppable." Dave Lombardo was relentless on the drums. And he only became more intense as the show went on. There are other bands that create a wall of sound that people describe as "brutal." It is just non-stop in your face guitars and full-blast double bass for four minutes at a time. To me, there's a limit where I just shut down and tune it out. It's maybe too much of a good thing. I am more impressed with a band that plays well musically, then has moments where they jump out and do something fast or crazy. Perhaps they build up to it. Either way, if you are looking to add musicality to what you're doing, it is important to allow the music to breathe a bit. Give the listener a moment to step back and appreciate what you're doing. It adds dynamics to the song and keeps things interesting.

You may have heard the saying about John Bonham that it wasn't what he played; it's what he *didn't* play that made him so good. He was one of the best at letting music breath, and it only added more to his groove. Don't get me wrong, one of my all-time favorite drumming moments is the fill he did after the first verse in "Achilles Last Stand." The point is, he knew when to get out of the way of the song and make room for the rest of the band.

GIVE THE BAND SOME SPACE

Be generous in your playing. Celebrate the other members of your band. Allow them to shine, as well. Don't feel that you have to dominate every bar of music you play. Sometimes it is best to cruise along and wait for an opening to jump out in the mix. Pick your moments and do something to stand out. Just make sure you allow the other band members the same courtesy. When you are playing fast, you may need to take a break, due to the physical demands of the song. Use that time to let your fellow band members have their moments. I've seen drummers who use every break in a song to do a crazy fast drum fill, and honestly, it gets a little repetitive. Remember, you should be able to justify every drum fill you play. Be selective, be tasteful, and be great!

PREPARATION VIDEO R

THINK ABOUT THE MIX—CONTROLLING YOUR DYNAMICS

When you are playing on your own, you may not be thinking about whether to play with your hi-hat open or closed. You may not be thinking about whether to ride on the bell of your ride cymbal or on one of your crashes. In a band situation, however, you need to think about the overall sound your band produces. What I mean is that each part of your kit produces different frequencies, as does each member of your band. The more the sound engineer can separate these frequencies, the cleaner the mix and the more everyone in the band can be heard. Also, the more definition in your playing, the more you'll be heard in the mix.

I once played a show where one of my peers was in the audience. Seeing him in the crowd was a great motivator and inspired me to play my absolute best. After the show, I was really satisfied with my playing and asked him what he thought. "You played great, but you need to close your hi-hat" was his response. After I got over the initial sting of his critique, I realized that playing with my hi-hat too open may have sounded fine to me, but it was washing out in the overall mix. What I needed to do was pay more attention to the way my playing sat in the mix, relative to the rest of the band. Playing with my hi-hat closed (not too much!) resulted in more definition and a much better groove for the band's overall sound.

When you're using speed mechanics and playing fast, the more definition you can add to your playing, the better. Otherwise, why play with high velocity if the listener can't hear what you're doing?

So look at the next few examples of different ways to play the same beat, with open hi-hat, closed hi-hat, crash ride, and ride cymbal. Listen to the video and notice how different the feel is in each application simply by altering my dynamics. In order that your highlight moments really jump out in the mix, you must learn to control your dynamics well, so as not to overpower your highlight. And the hi-hat is a huge part of this. Think about it this way: If you are playing on "10" all the time, where do you go to create a higher moment? Good, consistent control of your velocities on the metals (cymbals) will enable you to adjust your dynamics to make them ideal.

EXAMPLE VIDEO 65

Hi-Hat Control Exercise 65: Contrasting Open Hat Dynamics

Hi-Hat Control Exercise 66: Closed and Mid Hat Dynamics

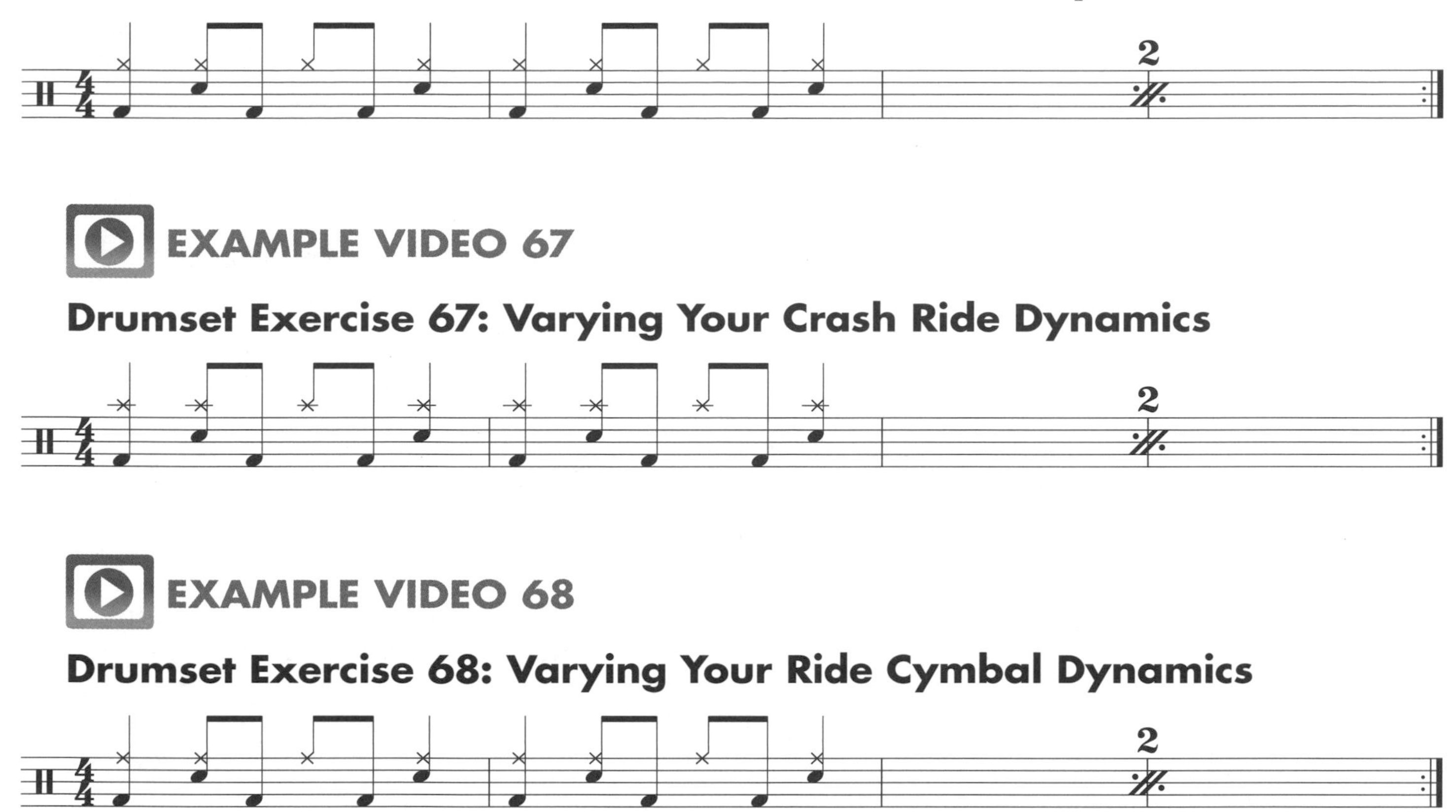

Triggers, Sound Replacement, and "Fix It in the Mix"

This has been a controversial subject for quite some time. I'm not saying *don't* employ these aids in your drumming; I'm merely suggesting not to use them as crutches. First, some explanation: Drum triggers (or simply "triggers") are devices that attach to the rim of a drum, with a small sensor that rests against the drumhead. Each time the drumhead is struck, the impact "triggers" the sensor, which sends a signal to a module (or "brain"). The module is programmed with different drum sounds, such as big bass drum with reverb, or clean bass drum with no effects for faster playing. Triggers can be placed on the snare drum and toms to use the programmed samples in the creation of pre-determined drum sounds or effects. When the module receives the signal, it sends out the programmed sound directly to the recording console (in a recording studio) or to a direct input (D/I) box, which then goes through the PA (in a live performance venue). The advantage to using triggers is that they send a clean signal directly into whatever sound system you're playing through. The sound is consistent and is easily manipulated or controlled.

Here's the problem: The sensitivity for triggers can be set very high, so all a drummer needs to do is barely tap the bass drum beater to the drumhead, and it can sound like a massive cannon shot. This has led to many drummers merely fluttering their feet on the pedals, and not really *playing drums*. The speed can be impressive, but it's certainly not very musical. For me, the goal is to play the same volume, whether I'm playing fast or slow (unless I'm playing softly to serve the song). If you listen to heavy music that has fast verses and breaks into half-time choruses, you'll notice that without triggers, the bass drum drops out of the mix in the fast double bass runs. This is because the drummer is not employing speed mechanics for drums! I stood in the wings at the Wiltern Theater in Los Angeles next to a famous drummer and watched him play blistering double bass with his band. From the audience perspective, he was playing the same volume, since the triggers were doing the work for him. However, from where I was standing, I could see and hear what he was *actually* playing. During the half-time parts, it sounded like normal drumming. But when it came to the double bass runs, I could barely hear him play. If he were using bass drum mics instead of triggers, his bass drums would have completely fallen out of the mix, unless the sound engineer brought up the volume of the bass drum channels every time there was a fast double bass run. My point is, it may be worth examining what you're really trying to accomplish when you must rely on technology to do the work for you in playing music. There are even bass drum pedals that deliver two hits to the bass drum for every one time the foot is pressed to the footboard. The idea is to double the drummer's bass drum speed. But does it really double the *drummer's* speed? More importantly, how does it serve the music?

I have used triggers on my bass drums in live performances, and they have served their purpose well. While watching a DVD of a show I played on the Sunset Strip, I noticed that the bass drum was suddenly missing in the mix. On the screen, I could see that the mic stand for the bass drum had swiveled so that the mic was nowhere near the hole in the front bass drum head. In fact, it had swung around and was pointing at the audience! Although it was funny to the guys in my band as we watched the performance, all I could think was, "Why did I work so hard on my double bass drumming if no one can even hear it?" I decided to take matters into my own hands and use triggers for the bass drums. That way, I had control over the sound going to the PA, as well as the quality of the tone. The only challenges with using triggers were dealing with the extra cables and module, and of course, the longer setup time required before our set.

These days, I've stopped using triggers altogether. The tone of my drumset is too good to replace with pre-programmed sounds. Acoustic drums are made to have their own sound, and it's up to the drummer to bring the tone out of them. We'll go into more depth on this subject later, but developing your own sound and vibe is a big part of distinguishing yourself from other drummers. When I was using triggers, it seemed like my sound was pretty much the same as everyone else who was using triggers. Think of it in terms of Neil Peart: When you hear him playing, you know it's Rush. Same with Alex Van Halen. These are drummers who worked hard in developing their own sound, their own vibe. In the Van Halen song "China Town," Alex played double bass at approximately 132 bpm. He could have triggered his bass drums for more definition, but the song is recorded entirely on an acoustic set, and it fits the song perfectly. Alex notoriously used drum pads and triggers in the mid 1980s—and a lot of the fans noticed a drastic change in his drum sound on the *5150* album, due to it having been recorded using drum pads and triggers. Alex has amazing feel in his playing, and drummers in particular claimed he lost some of that feel by abandoning acoustic drums in that period.

On a related note, sound replacement is often used in the studio to make the drummer sound "better," but what does that really mean? I was asked to do a session for a band in which they had a drumset mic'ed up in a studio, and my job was to "walk in and nail it." I played the kit and asked for some time to tune it properly. The producer/engineer replied that there was no need to tune it because they were going to use sound replacement. What that meant was, they would replace every single drum hit with a pre-sampled drum sound. If you look at drum tracks on a computer screen, you can see that each track has its own set of drum hits. Using plug-ins from the recording software, the engineer can replace each hit with any drum sound they want. As you can imagine, this leads to drum tones that don't even belong to the drummer; they actually belong to someone else! Whoever they're sampling is the one providing the real drum tones. Drumming isn't just *what* you play, it's *how* you play it. That's the true nature behind drum tones. If someone plays lightly when they play fast, the sound replacement can make it sound as though they're pounding the drums like an animal. Not to take anything away from recording engineers; they are the backbone of any good recording and are a vital part of the recording process, but in terms of artistry, giving an honest representation of how the drummer *really* plays is the way to deliver the human element to any recording. So if you are the drummer, it's your responsibility to know how to make your drums and drumming sound so good that little, if any, studio treatment needs to be applied to your drum tracks. That, to me, is the ideal situation.

On the other hand, sound replacement can be a useful tool when used sparingly. For example, if the drummer executes a drum fill that needs a little more definition in the mix, a good engineer may bring in a small amount of sound replacement to give it a boost. In that case, it helps the overall sound. Where things get out of hand is when the engineer uses sound replacement on *every* fill, or on the entire track, for that matter. Don't seek to use sound replacement as a crutch in your playing.

One of the biggest crutches drummers use is when they ask the engineer to "fix it in the mix." What that means is, if the drummer makes a mistake while recording, that mistake can be remedied or "fixed" by the engineer. For example, if the drummer does a fast double bass run and one of the hits is late or is missed entirely, the engineer can either move that hit and fix it, or add a hit where one didn't exist before, all with a few simple clicks. If minimal fixes are required, no big deal; this is something that is actually very common in the recording world. Where problems arise is when drummers begin relying on things to be fixed in the mix, as opposed to doing the work and not making those mistakes in the first place. Studio time is costly; you may be working with a limited budget that doesn't allow for multiple takes. If you want your drum tracks to sound their best, you need to be sure you put the time into your preproduction work so you arrive at the studio prepared to record your parts with precision and consistency.

On "Kaleidoscope" I recorded the drums for that song in one single take; no punching in, no triggers, and no fixes. Many drummers are accustomed to recording a section of a song, stopping, and then punching in again where they left off. "Kaleidoscope" was recorded as one continuous take. That meant that if I made a mistake, I had to start over from the beginning and play the song all the way through with no mistakes. Most of my musician and engineer friends think I'm crazy, but this is the way I record pretty much everything, this way there is one continuous vibe throughout the track. There are no changes in feel or tone. It takes longer to do it this way, but the end result feels more real and authentic to me.

"KALEIDOSCOPE"

Finally, let's put your new skills to the test! The following song incorporates the exercises and concepts throughout *Speed Mechanics for Drums* at 170 bpm. It also explores a range of styles throughout its dynamic and mood changes, as well as some quite progressive time shifts.

After you learn it, identify those moments that are particularly difficult for you, break them down as you've seen me do it throughout this book, and then reassemble them. Also, create your own variations!

I am a lefty, so I tend to lead with my stronger left hand. So if you are right-handed, you will sometimes want to use opposite sticking patterns. In some cases, that can create awkward arm crossing situations. Again, the simplest way to transform any pattern into a comfortable, non-crossing, right-handed lead is simply to swap each floor tom for the rack tom, and each rack tom for the floor tom. This will give a similar texture, as it allows you to keep the snare drum in the exact same place. This is one way to deal with it. Another way is to keep in mind that it is also beneficial to challenge yourself to lead with your weak hand on occasion. And of course, there is always the option of changing the pattern altogether to better suit you. If you happen to have additional toms in your set, you may further adapt these fills and patterns.

Consider my performance here as a "framework" to adapt and experiment with. This left/right issue may seem to add an extra degree of difficulty, but I really think it is beneficial: It forces you to think for yourself a little more and adapt my ideas into your own playing, rather than simply copying them. Remember, the real goal isn't to learn to play this song itself as I did, but rather, to develop all the required skills and speed mechanics, and then to make it your own!

Video example 69 shows my performance of "Kaleidoscope." Then for video example 70, you will have the drum tracks muted and hear just the *click* along with all guitar and bass (and co-author Troy Stetina performing the lead guitar track). This is done so that you can put on headphones and play along with the band. Enjoy!

EXAMPLE VIDEOS 69, 70
Kaleidoscope
BY CHRIS MOORE AND TROY STETINA
A
0:04
Intro (Theme 1)
♩ = 170
Played with double strokes
rims
3
5
7
6
B
0:15
Intro 2 (Drums)
9
11
(Quads from hell)
13
15
C
0:27
Theme 2
17

19
21
23
D
0:38
Theme 3
25
27
29
31
E
0:49
Breakdown 1
33
37

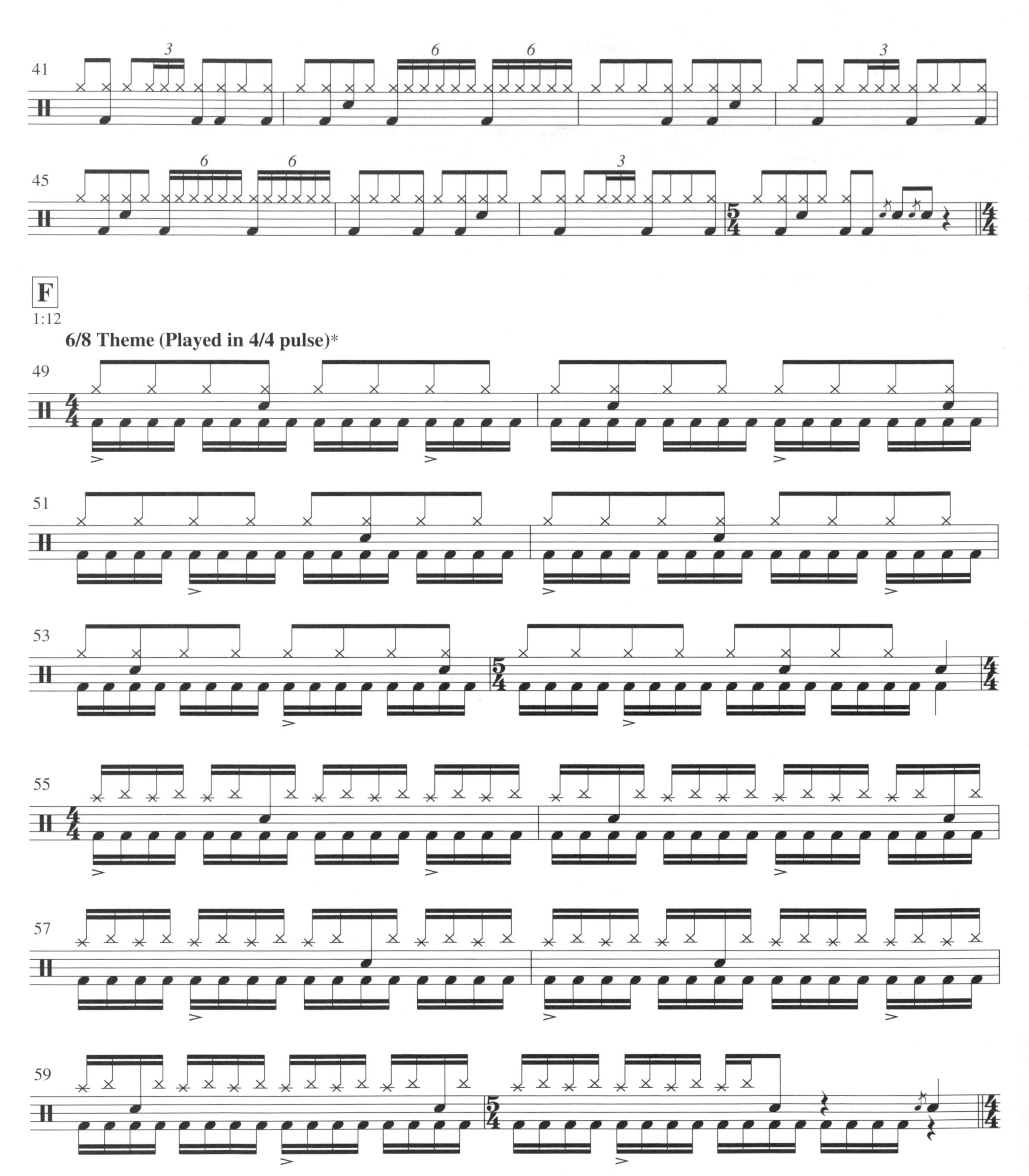

*If you regard the accented kicks and snare hits as indicating 6/8 feel, that pulse in 6/8 would equal 113 bpm. That is, the "common denominator" is an eighth note, at 170 bpm x 2, = 340, and 340 ÷ 3 eighths per compound beat in 6/8 = 113 bpm. It is, however, written here in 4/4 at 170 bpm throughout because at measure 54, we see an extra beat of ♫ value, which is easy to get if you are counting in 4/4, but difficult in 6/8. This is a very progressive approach, using the 4/4 – 6/8 interplay.

G
1:30
Interlude
Play 3x
61
6
6
63
6
H
1:41
Theme 1 (Reprise)
65
67
69
71
I
1:52
Theme 3
73
75

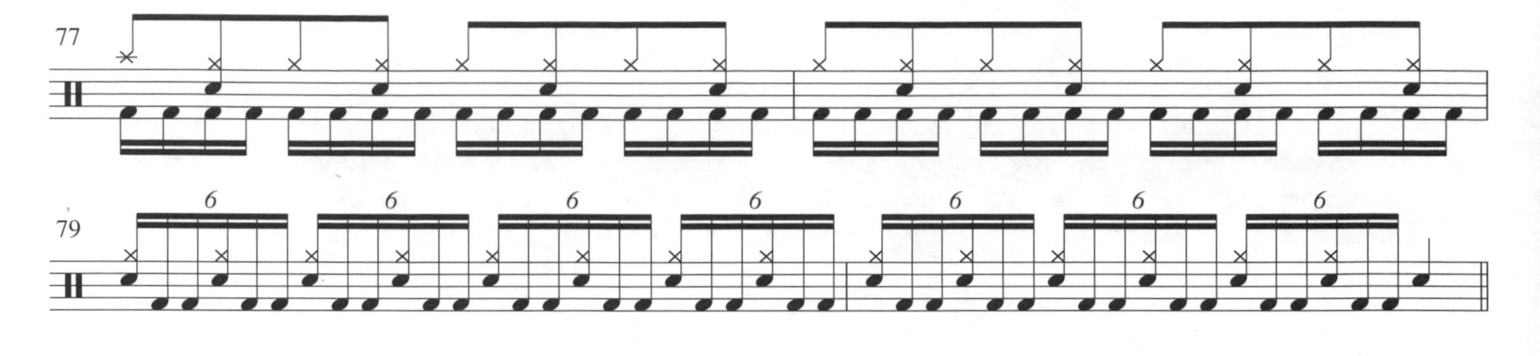
77
79

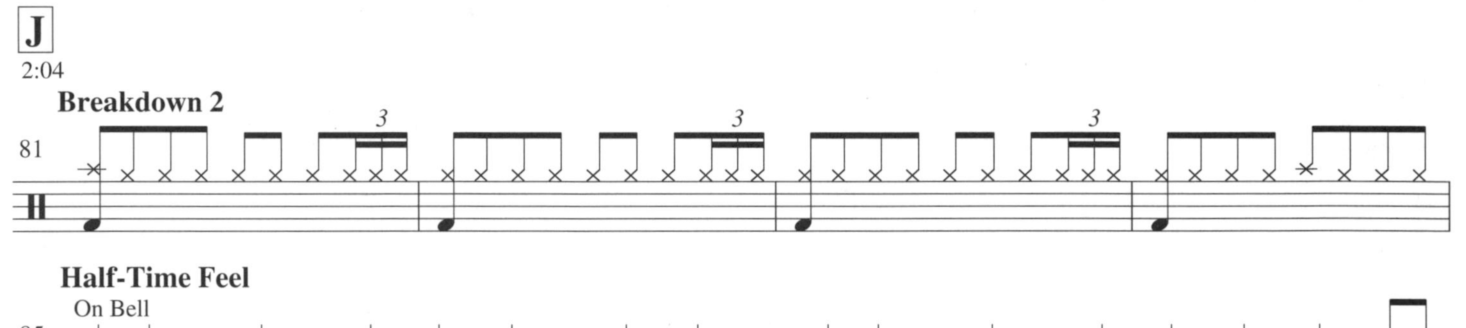
J
2:04
Breakdown 2
81

Half-Time Feel
On Bell
85
89
92

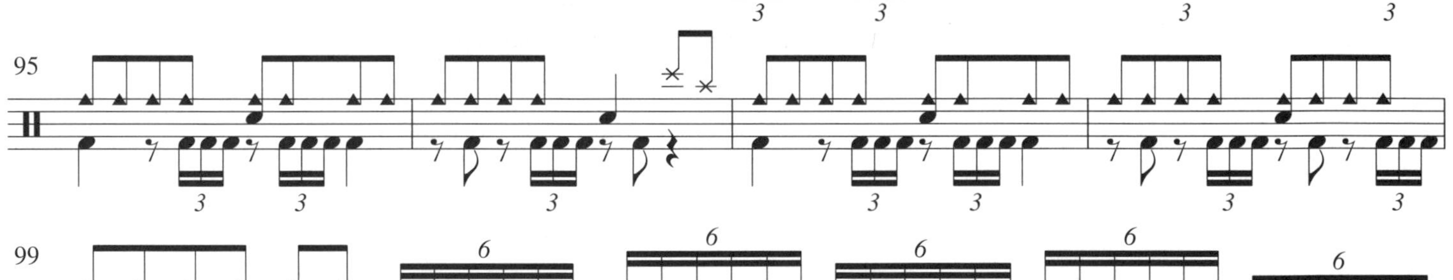
95

99

101

*At measures 117–118, we return to the 6/8 feel. Here, each set of three sixteenths equals half of the compound 6/8 meter, the crash emphasizing the guitar chords playing ♩. 𝄽. ♩. 𝄽. pattern (note, rest, note, rest). Again, this progressive switch to temporary 6/8 feel has been notated in 4/4 for ease of performance.

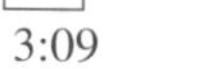

L
3:09
Theme 3
127
129
131
133
M
3:20
Breakdown 3
135
Half Time ♩ = 85
Sixteenth Shuffle Feel
139
141
143

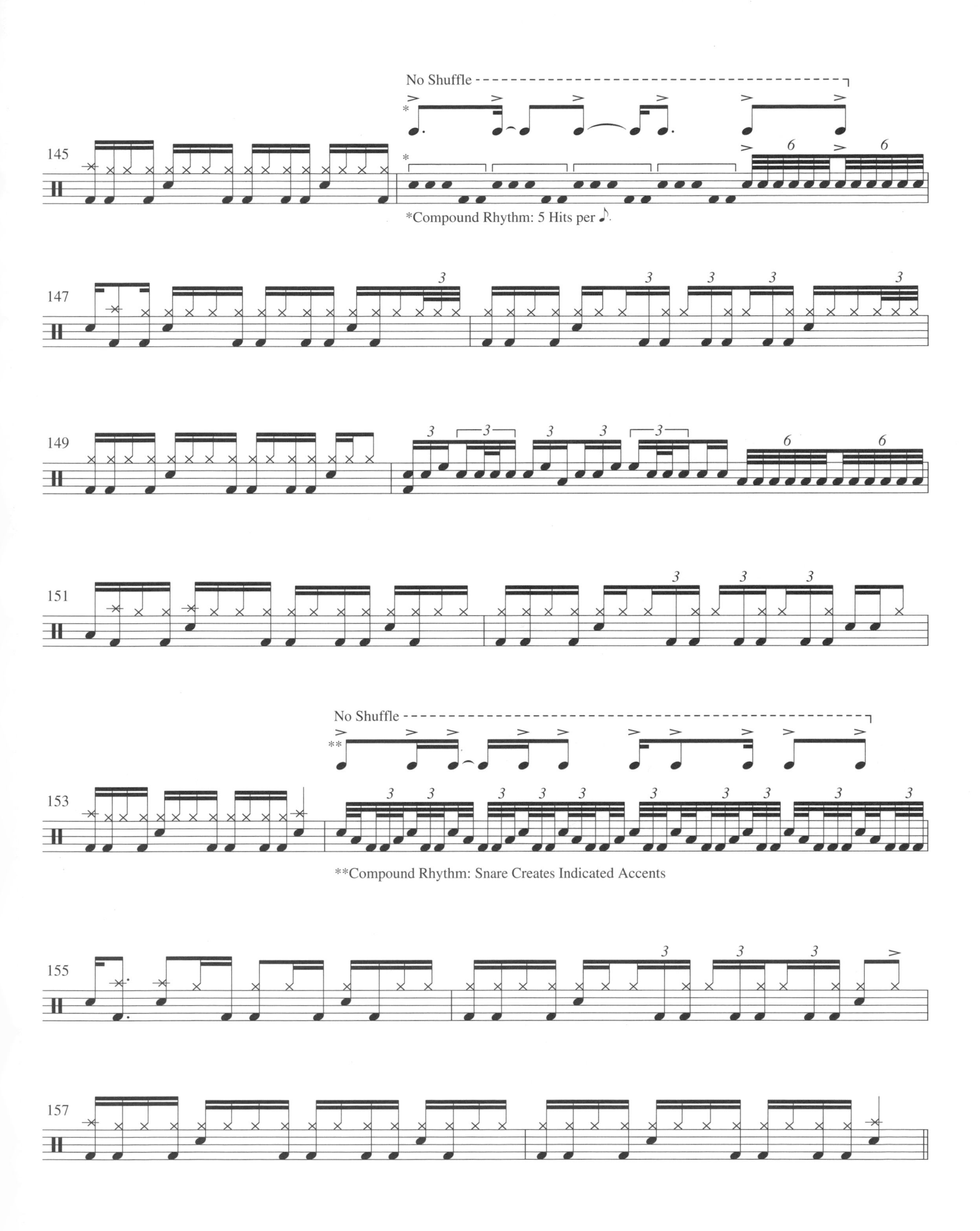
No Shuffle
145
*Compound Rhythm: 5 Hits per ♪.
147
149
151
No Shuffle
153
**Compound Rhythm: Snare Creates Indicated Accents
155
157

N
4:22
"Coda" (Long Build)
♩ = 170
159
*Double Stroke Snares
162
1.
2.
164
167
169
172
O
4:56
Theme 1 (Reprise)
174
177
180

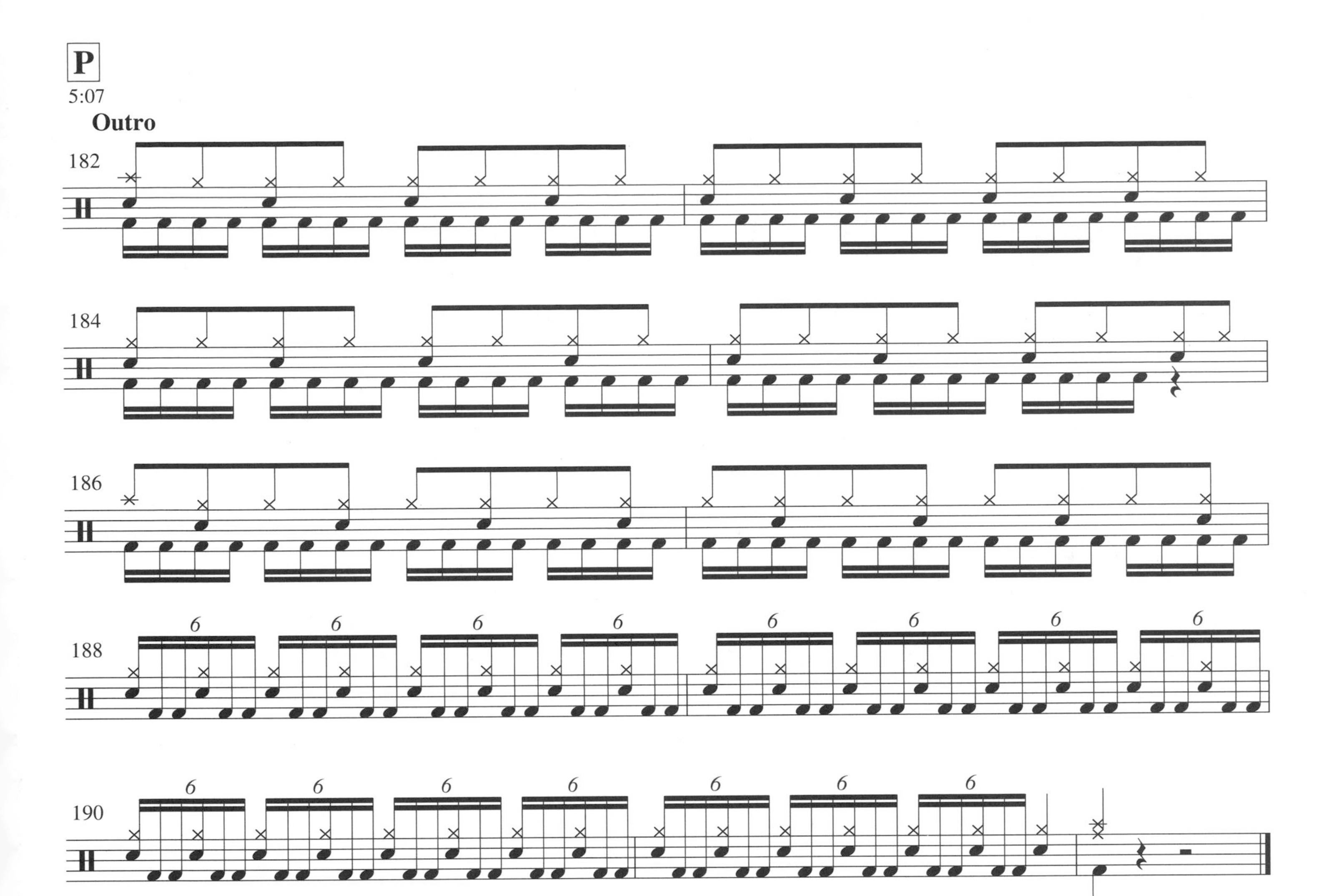
P
5:07
Outro
182
184
186
188
6
190

CLOSING THOUGHTS

Thank you for taking the time to invest in your skillset through *Speed Mechanics for Drums*. Using the concepts and exercises from this book and video, my hope is that you will improve your speed and accuracy on the drumset, become a more holistic musician, and accomplish your goals in drumming and in music. Refer back to this book whenever you hit a plateau in your playing or need to refresh your skills. You may also have certain exercises that develop into your favorite drum fills, or certain key phrases from the text that become your mantra as you play. These are the sacred elements that belong to *only* you and make up who you are as a musician. Truly, being able to share this knowledge and experience with you is a dream come true. I hope to see you at a show or a drum clinic sometime! I leave with this: Remember that you can accomplish anything you want on the drums… all it takes is practice. Dream big!